BORGES

AND EUROPE

REVISITED

Edited by

Evelyn Fishburn

Institute of Latin American Studies
31 Tavistock Square, London WC1H 9HA

Institute of Latin American Studies
School of Advanced Study
University of London

British Library Cataloguing-in-Publication Data
A catalogue record for this book is available
from the British Library

ISBN   1 900039 21 4

CONTENTS

Acknowledgements

I must start by expressing due appreciation to the Institute of Romance Studies, the Institute of Latin American Studies, the British Academy and the University of North London who all gave generous support to the organisation of the one day conference upon which most of the chapters in this volume are based and also to Simona Cain for her friendly guidance and expertise. I would like to thank particularly the chairs of the different panels for their helpful interventions and for their able promotion of lively debate at the end of each session.

I should like to give special thanks to John King for the unstinting generosity with which he encouraged and supported this project from the moment of its inception to completion and for his practical advice throughout. Finally, my greatest debt of gratitude is to Tony Bell for his careful and intelligent contribution to this edition and for imposing order and coherence upon it.

List of Contributors

Malcolm Bowie is Marshal Foch Professor of French Literature at the University of Oxford and a Fellow of All Souls. His publications include books on Michaux, Mallarmé and Lacan. His book *Proust Among the Stars* (HarperCollins) appeared in 1998.

Daniel Balderston is the head of the Spanish department at the University of Iowa. His publications include three books on Borges: *El precursor velado: R. L. Stevenson en la obra de Borges* (Sudamericana, 1985), *The Literary Universe of Jorge Luis Borges* (Greenwood, 1986) and *Out of Context: Historical Reference and the Representation of Reality in Borges* (Duke University Press, 1993; Spanish edition, Beatriz Viterbo Editora, 1996).

Evelyn Fishburn is Professor of Latin American Literary Studies at the University of North London and Associate Fellow of the Institute of Latin American Studies. She has led a post-graduate seminar on Borges (and Cortázar) at the University of London for many years. She co-authored *A Dictionary of Borges* (Duckworth, 1990) with Psiche Hughes and has published extensively on different aspects of Borges's work. Her other publications include a book on immigration in Argentine literature (Bibliotheca Ibero-Americana, 1981), an edited collection of short stories by Spanish American Women (Manchester University Press, 1998) and various articles on women writers. Currently, she is working on Humour. Evelyn Fishburn convened the Conference 'Borges and European Culture', held at the Institute of Romance Studies in conjunction with the Institute of Latin American Studies in May 1996, on which the present collection of essays is based.

Gabriel Josipovici is Professor of English in the School of European Studies at the University of Sussex. He is the author of eleven novels, two volumes of short stories and a number of critical works.

Bernard McGuirk is Professor of Romance Literatures and Literary Theory at the University of Nottingham, where he is also Head of the Postgraduate School of Critical Theory. He is currently President of the Association of Hispanists of Great Britain and Ireland (1996-98). He has published widely on French, Spanish, Portuguese and Latin American Literatures. His recent books include *Reconceptions. Reading Modern French Poetry* (edited with Russell King, University of Nottingham, 1996), *Latin American Literature: Symptoms, Risks and Strategies of Post-Structuralist Criticism* (Routledge, 1996), and *Retranslating Latin America: Dimensions of the Third Term* (edited with Else Vieira, in press).

Sylvia Molloy is Albert Schweitzer Professor of the Humanities at New York University. Her publications include *La Diffusion de la littérature hispano-*

américaine en France au XXe siècle (Presses Universitaires de France, 1972), *La letras de Borges* (Sudamericana, 1979), *En breve cárcel* (novel, Seix Barral, 1981), *At Face Value: Autobiographical Writing in Spanish America* (Cambridge University Press, 1991) and many essays on 19th- and 20th- century Latin American literatures and cultures. She is also co-editor of *Women's Writing in Latin America* (Westview Press, 1991) and co-editor of *Hispanisms and Homosexualities* (forthcoming, 1998). She is currently working on a book on decadence and the construction of sexualities in turn-of-the-century Latin America and writing a second novel.

Eduardo L. Ortiz is Professor of Mathematics and of the History of Mathematics at Imperial College, London; Professeur de la Première Classe, Université d'Orléans, France, 1992-93; Foreign Fellow, National Academy of Sciences, Buenos Aires, 1988; Foreign Fellow, Royal Academy of Sciences, Madrid, 1990; J. Babini History of Science National Prize, Argentina, 1990; Chief Editor, The Humboldt Library, London. He was John Simon Guggenheim Research Fellow in the Department of History at Harvard University from 1996-98.

William Rowe is Professor of Latin American Cultural Studies at King's College London. He has published six books on Latin American literature and culture, including (with Vivian Schelling) *Memory and Modernity:Popular Culture in Latin America* London (Verso, 1991); *Hacia una poética radical: ensayos de hermenéutica cultural* (Beatriz Viterbo and Mosca Azul, 1996); *Ensayos arguedianos* (Universidad de San Marcos and Sur, 1996). William Rowe is co-ordinator of the Centre for Latin American Cultural Studies at King's College London.

Jason Wilson is Professor of Latin American Literature at University College, London. His publications include *Octavio Paz: A Study of his Poetics* (Cambridge University Press, 1979); *Octavio Paz* (Twayne Publishers, 1986); *An A-Z of Modern Latin American Literature in English Translation* (Institute of Latin American Studies, 1989); *Traveller's Literary Companion to South & Central America* (In Print, 1993). He has edited and translated Alexandre von Humboldt's *Personal Narrative of a Journey to the Equinoctial Regions of the New Continent* for Penguin Classics (1995), and written numerous articles on Hispanic poetry and travel writing. He is completing a cultural history of Buenos Aires, and his study of literary travellers in Latin American is forthcoming: *Parables of Travel: Imagining and Misinterpreting Latin America.*

Introduction

Evelyn Fishburn

This is a compilation of essays taking a fresh look at Borges's work. The word 'Europe' in the title is taken in its widest sense, as the central and authoritative mental space within which and against which 'World' literature was written at the time of Borges's formative years. The present collection was not conceived as an overview of Borges's relationship with Europe but as an eclectic response by different authors with different interests to a subject that had become importantly refocused. A wide variety of topics, ranging from the European avant-garde to the impact of European science upon Argentine literature, is discussed from a multiplicity of angles, the only unifying factor being the year 1996, when nearly all the essays were written. Most of them were presented as papers at a one-day conference held at the Institute of Romance Studies, in conjunction with the Institute of Latin American Studies, London University. The purpose was to re-examine the work of Borges in the wake of the great changes in reading that 'theory' had brought about and which Borges had somehow foreshadowed, though, of course, not systematised.

The title acknowledges this change in perception. Of particular significance were the ideas of structuralism, freeing the work from its genesis; deconstruction, freeing it from the tyranny of 'meaning' and, perhaps most relevantly, cultural studies and post colonialism, the first returning, but with a difference, to evaluate cultural context and the second raising hybridity from its bastard status to a position of prominence. These issues are discussed with unsurprising foresight in 'El escritor argentino y la tradición' ['The Argentine Writer and Tradition'] (1925), an essay which in recent years has achieved something approximating cult status. In the early years Borges owed recognition of his genius to international acclaim. It was not until critics such as Drieu la Rochelle declared him, in Michelin guide style, to be 'worth the journey' that his recognition was secured in his country, yet one cannot help feeling that the journey Drieu had in mind was to the Parisian bookshops, not to remote Argentina.[1] In those still heavily Eurocentric days, if Borges merited recognition it was because he was Mainstream, which was understood to mean European or European-style and which was almost synonymous with Universal.[2]

But to be branded European was a double-edged accolade in Argentina, for if

---

[1]   Borges was aware of this prejudice as is made clear in his eulogy of Paul Groussac. See *Discusión* (Buenos Aires Emecé, 1957), p. 95

[2]   It in interesting to note the original title of an important critical work on Latin-American literature by Luis Harss, *Into the Mainstream* (New York: Harper & Row, 1967), translated into Spanish as *Los nuestros* (Buenos Aires· Sudamericana, 1973)

part of the country admired him for his cosmopolitanism, another vilified him for his lack of national consciousness. Borges has mostly produced very intelligent readings and no hint of disparagement should be construed into the foregoing observations: they were right for the time when they were made. The details of the debate are not of interest here as much as the changed readings that have ensued in the last twenty or thirty years, and what they tell us about ourselves: '... si me fuera otorgado leer cualquier página actual – ésta, por ejemplo – como la leerán el año dos mil, yo sabría cómo será la literatura el año dos mil' [If I were able to read any contemporary page – this one, for example – as it would be read in the year 2000, I would know what literature would be like in the year 2000] wrote Borges in 'Una nota para (hacia) Bernard Shaw' [For Bernard Shaw][3]. As the year 2000 approaches it is timely to read Borges afresh with this aim in mind.

The opening essay by Sylvia Molloy sets the tone for the collection by reassessing notions of totality in Borges. Recalling famous misreadings of history, and highlighting the failure of 'translating' meaning from one culture to another, she discusses different aspects of transculturation, putting forward the view that Borges consistently problematised cultural polarities which assumed a stable subject position from which 'difference' could be argued. Her illustrative example is taken from 'El evangelio según Marcos' [The Gospel According to Mark], a story which is based upon the tragic misunderstanding by a peasant family of the message in Mark's Gospel as read by a young medical student from Buenos Aires. The point Molloy argues is that, like all notions of totality, the 'natural' polarisation between European and native expected in a Latin American setting is overturned by the fact that both parties, of mixed ancestry, are culturally hybrid. European readings of Third World Literature are generally reductive, ironing out local specificity in order to fit into a pre-established rhetoric of 'otherness'. (Alternatively, they seek, and find, confirmation of an assumed exotica such as the presumed 'documentary' merit of Magic Realism would indicate.) Whereas European critical reception of Borges either used him to exemplify pre-established ideas of a stereotype or sought to understand him separately from his rich cultural context, Borges, for his part, contrived to dismantle the rhetoric of 'otherness'. One way of doing so was by 'democratically' mixing allusions to classical culture with allusions to practically unknown Argentine writers and texts and by drawing comparisons between popular local aphorisms with maxims found in such pre-eminent writers as Shakespeare and Gracián. This irreverent border-crossing dismantles accepted hierarchies and invites new positions from which to read old texts. Molloy's point is not so much to 'castigate' European-based reductions and simplifications as to explore the inescapably transient and ever enriching complexities of all cultural expressions.

Borges's resistance to notions of totality is discussed from a different

---

[3]   *Otras inquisiciones* (Buenos Aires· Emecé, 1952), p. 218; *Other Inquisitions* (Austin and London. University of Texas Press, 1965)

perspective by William Rowe who focuses on national and cultural boundaries, showing them to be time-bound artificial entities. The example given is that of Europe where what constituted the frontier between east and west before the Second World War is dramatically different from our understanding of these demarcation lines today. His focus is on history and nationhood, discussed through an experimental reading of 'El jardín de senderos que se bifurcan' [The Garden of Forking Paths], set in Europe at the time of World War two when frontiers were being re-negotiated. Totality in Borges is always dissolved, either because, as in Ts'ui Pên's story there is a residual meaning even in the wake of complete success or because, as in 'La escritura del Dios' [The God's Script], the experience of plenitude renders isolated meanings irrelevant. The old notion of Europe, as represented in the nationalistic endeavours of Yu Tsun is made ironic by a subplot of an eternally bifurcating novel, an image that recalls the eternal relocation of frontiers (and meanings).

In his reading of 'Funes el memorioso' [Funes the Memorious] set in the River Plate, in the nation-forming decade of the 1880s, nationhood is linked to time. The story evokes a time when the Argentinian frontier with the 'desert' and the 'savage' ceased to be porous and the state became consolidated. Two perceptions of time, one chronological, the other chaotic, exist in Funes's mind, refusing synthesis. The same can be said about his memory: total recall, impossible to classify. Both these images are read as metaphors of a totalitarian state and its bureaucratic organisation.

The porosity of Borges's hyperallusive text to European cultural references creates what Rowe calls 'a reading machine', producing endless rereadings. For example, read from a novel by Saer, 'Funes' is a machine that can make holes in the formation of a nation-state, but read from a poem by Celan it becomes an exploration of the collision between language and inherited meanings.

Like Molloy, Rowe draws conclusions about the instability of every place from which to read.

Daniel Balderston's essay also relates to the questioning of notions of totality, this time concerning Borges's understanding of classical or canonical literature. Balderston's essay develops in polemical dialogue with Harold Bloom's writings on the subject.

Harold Bloom is a masterful reader, brilliant in his insights, persuasive in his enthusiasm. But he is also an unashamedly prescriptive critic: so much is clear about someone who not only offers his selection of 'the Western canon', but who cursorily dismisses anyone who might find any of these three terms ('the', 'Western' and 'canon') problematical, banning them to what he calls the School of Resentment. His reading of Borges captures much of what is important and pays tribute to those aspects of Borges that find favour with his view of what literature ought to be, but there are serious shortcomings too. For these he is taken to task by Balderston whose essay discusses the idea of canon and

Borges's handling of the subject, placing Borges's ideas against Bloom's. Where Bloom seeks to anchor his chosen texts, Borges points to a ubiquitous centre, always on the move according to the time, place, and particularity of the reader. Balderston, in an interpretation of 'La busca de Averroes' which disguises the irony of its findings, sees Averroes's defeat (his trouble with understanding the term 'tragedy' as used by Aristotle) 'cast as a tragedy in Aristotle's terms'. He examines the means by which this story is arguing directly against any notion of a universal text, supporting his findings by his own reading of Averroes. Lack of universality need not be taken as totally negative: though Aristotle was misunderstood through multiple translations in the Arab world, as was Averroes in the West, misreadings, and particularly cultural misreadings, can still act as enriching forms of communication. The repetition of a metaphor need not be a descent into cliché but may open up into multiplied meanings. It is on the point of repeated readings of Borges that Bloom and Balderston stand furthest apart, the former finding re-reading Borges a limited experience whilst for the latter it is every time entering into 'undiscovered country'.

The notion of a subverted canon has been applied yet again to Borges, this time to his use of allusion. In the weighty words of Antoine Compagnon, 'Borges revèle le negatif du fonctionnement canonique de la citation'.[4] The process of this negative canonicity is, however, double-edged. Borges uses allusions paradoxically, as a refuge, a hiding behind an accepted and authoritative cultural tradition. Mostly, this is the tradition of 'Europe' in the extended sense of this volume. Then, emboldened, the refuge is upturned. 'Heresy', 'sacrilege', 'perversion', are some of the admiring qualifiers used by critics regarding the daring and idiosyncratic use Borges makes of so many allusions.

In 'Hidden Pleasures in the Allusions of Borges' I focus mainly on the many different ways in which allusion can be made to function in readings of Borges. I seek to establish no overarching theory but note, instead, a variety of 'ploys', from the throwaway veiled allusion for a few initiates, to those that give a particular entry to a story or act as an encapsulating metaphor of it. Of particular fascination are those where only the source reference is given and which, when the reference is chased back to its origin, reveals hitherto hidden meanings which stand in ironic contrast to more traditional interpretations.

Moving on to the question of Borges's concept of reality, it could be said that the mirror that the heresiarch of Uqbar found abominable may well have been the one paraded along the road by Stendhal, the mirror of Realism;[5] if so, Borges would have concurred, since he believed Realism to be one of the heresies of our time. But not so reality. Gabriel Josipovici's understanding of the message of what he considers one of Borges's greatest stories, 'Tlön, Uqbar,

---

[4]   Antoine Compagnon, *La Seconde main ou le travail de la citation* (Paris· Editions du Seuil, 1979).

[5]   'Un miroir qu'on promène le long d'un chemin', epigraph to Chapter XIII of *Le Rouge et le noir*

Orbis Tertius', is that we have only one life and that every moment is precious.

Josipovici's careful summary brings to light the process by which *hrönir* are created and which the story emulates: an entry on Uqbar is found, willed into existence, lost, and when found again it has become magnified into an entire volume. Similarly, the world, like a *hron* re-shaped by expectations and desires for harmony, has become more coherent, more harmonious, more certain. In short: totalitarian and Tlön. The only point of resistance is in the stoic effort of the narrator to pursue a pointless task in defence of reality as it is. The reality that Borges celebrates here, however, differs from the false reality of the realist novel, where causality is 'heretically' inserted in order to make the lifelike meaningful (a point adding a different perspective to Borges's discussion in 'El arte narrativo y la magia' ['The Art of Narrative and Magic']). Josipovici evokes Kierkegaard's ideas on 'actuality' (that the actual cannot be conceived because to do so dissolves it into possibility) to shed light on Borges's views on a reality 'unfalsified by the imagination'. Reality in its uniqueness is what Wallace Stevens has termed 'the plain sense of things': the wonder of the 'now' is not that it should be the only way possible, as insinuated in the realist novel, but that it should be as it is and not as in all the possibilities of the imagination. This reading enriches our understanding of Borges's sombre realist credo, 'el mundo, desgraciadamente, es real; yo, desgraciadamente soy Borges' [The world, unfortunately, is real; I, unfortunately, am Borges].[6]

Poetry is the genre discussed in the next two essays. In the first, Jason Wilson focuses on early influences, shedding new light on Borges's known hostility towards surrealism, particularly in its Parisian-based deliberations, and the effect this had upon his own poetics. In spite of having written a few early militant poems (which he soon repudiated), Borges felt pronounced hostility towards the Paris-based avant-garde, particularly as it became more politically committed in its search for a new aesthetics. Speculating on the reasons why Borges may have misunderstood the surrealist idea of perennial renovation, Wilson examines some crucial notions that separate Borges and Surrealism such as 'revolution', 'dream', 'love' and 'the surrealist tradition'. Renovation for Borges did not mean changing the world by changing both man and art but, following the lead from the Hispanic (and German) avant-garde, the search in his poetry was for a new style, simply a move away from tradition and from the influence of poets like Darío and Lugones. Wilson sees Borges's increasing poetic timidity, what he calls his 'poet's block' (Borges wrote very little poetry between 1929 and 1960), as stemming from his realisation that he was 'condemned' to being 'a speculative poet', sincere, anachronistic and private.

Most critics hold the view that Surrealism, which Borges detested, had no influence upon his poetry, but Wilson's thesis is that far from simply ignoring the movement, his distaste for 'the radical French tradition' had the effect of making him retreat into an essentialised position. Poetry meant something very

---

[6] *Otras inquisiciones*, p 256, *Other Inquisitions*, p 187.

private to Borges and his antipathy towards the political aspirations of the surrealist movement helped him to define his own, different, way of being a poet. Therefore it is ironic that possibly the first poem to deal with the South Atlantic conflict should have been Borges's 'Juan López y John Ward'.

In Bernard McGuirk's self-avowedly poststructuralist essay poetry is looked at from a very different perspective. McGuirk examines questions of translation and cultural difference by situating Borges's poem in various contexts. The first places 'Juan López y John Ward' against Wilfred Owen's earlier poem 'Strange Meeting', analysing both texts in the light of recent poststructuralist thinking on the question of history and excess in writing. A later poem, the Argentine Susana Thénon's 'Poema con traducción simultánea Español-Español' is contrasted with Borges's poem in terms of the protocols of restraint and propriety. Finally, Tony Conran's 'Elegy for the Welsh Dead, in the Falklands Islands, 1982' is considered within a Celtic 'boundary' tradition of the search for national identity without the glories of patriotism. At each point of the analyses, Borges's poem serves as a filter for the theoretical argument that 'the *question* of history is excessive with respect to history', Geoffrey Bennington's version of the need to interrogate all history. The capacity of Borges and other writers to appropriate and, at the same time, to lay bare the doubts upon which earlier traditions of war poetry often rest is compared to the intellectual and aesthetic processes of translation. Finally, in a reading of Borges's 'Milonga del muerto' [Milonga of the Dead Man'], the gap between historical reality and its written representation is poignantly laid bare.

Eduardo Ortiz's essay stands on its own: its purpose is to review the place of science in the formative process of the nation, and assess its role in the literary imagination. Contrary to commonly held views regarding the complete dominance of Scientism and particularly Positivism in Argentina, and indeed throughout the Latin-American continent, Ortiz argues that a strong metaphysical legacy dating from as far back as the hermetic writings of the Catalan Raimond Llull lived on, becoming the substratum to Positivistic thought. The developments of new physics in nineteenth-century Europe reached Argentina largely filtered through Spanish science, and ideas about infinity, space, and time were widely discussed among the academic and intellectual elite. Borges's forefather, Lafinur, was instrumental in giving due prominence to scientific thought in academic teaching.[7] The visit that Einstein made to Argentina in 1925 – which has received so little critical attention – marked the culmination of the process of rapid advance described earlier, clearly producing an impact that exceeded the boundaries of pure science. Lugones's vital role in organising this visit cannot be overrated, and the specific example of his poetry is used to illustrate the sympathetic relations that existed between scientists, writers and poets at that time. But his use of a transformed scientific imaginary separates him from Borges. Ortiz is not overconcerned with tracing direct links between Borges's work and scientific ideas – though when he does

---

[7] *Otras inquisiciones*, p. 236.

so his comments are fascinating – but seeks rather, most convincingly, to argue for an intellectual background that made the abstract thoughts of Borges seem totally at home.

The Afterword by Malcolm Bowie is a tribute to Borges, capturing the essential and distinguishing features of his art. Allusion is the means by which Borges gives his own sparse prose 'its constant air of plenitude'; it is his link to the past and his reaching outwards, to the vibrancy of life, real and imagined. 'Hablar es caer en tautologías' [To speak is to resort to tautology] wrote Borges, famously, pointing out the self-referentiality of all thought and writing, but, as Bowie remarks, 'the writer of fiction has the unenviable task of making something new from other people's litter'. This Borges does, not only with other people's 'litter' but with his own. Stories which most repeat previous plots, renew themselves in unexpected ways.

It is fitting, in the context of the present volume, that Bowie's final tribute to Borges should be set against the backdrop of Valéry who for Borges was 'a symbol of Europe and its delicate twilight'. Borges paid tribute to Valéry's 'pure spirit', considering the poet even greater than his work; Bowie contrasts the pure intellect of the French poet with Borges's. In his juxtaposition of the two writers Bowie emphasises aspects of Borges that have remained unacknowledged too long (though they are perhaps hinted at in Josipovici's essay): his dispersal of selfhood and yet vibrant immersion in life. 'Borges inhabits literature as one might inhabit a great city – surprised by its curiosities, pausing at its crossroads, crossing and recrossing its thoroughfares endlessly, switching from its surface to its underground routes, and never wanting it to be a single portentous thing.'

CHAPTER 1

Lost in Translation: Borges, the Western Tradition and Fictions of Latin America

Sylvia Molloy

In a scene, highlighted in many Latin American history books, which definitely left a trace in my memory as I was growing up in Argentina, Atahualpa, the Inca emperor, tragically brings on his own downfall and that of his people. When presented by Pizarro's chaplain with a bible (or the chaplain's breviary: the chroniclers cannot agree) the Inca prince casts the book to the ground. Willfully interpreting such a gesture as sacrilegious, and oblivious to the fact that the 'book', as cultural artifact, cannot be recognised by Atahualpa because it does not exist within his system of representation, the Spaniards (so the legend goes) then proceed to redress this unforgivable affront by imprisoning the Inca and waging war on his subjects. The cry of remonstrance attributed to Pizarro's chaplain by Garcilaso is eloquent: '¡Cristianos, los Evangelios hollados! ¡Justicia y venganza sobre éstos! ¡Ea, ea, destruidlos, que menosprecian nuestra ley y no quieren nuestra amistad!'[1] – ['Christians, the Gospels dashed to the ground! Justice and vengeance for them! Come, let us kill them for they belittle our law and shun our friendship'] the chaplain is supposed to have exclaimed. What Atahualpa 'belittles' is *las escrituras* but, more generally, all forms of *escritura*. Not only *scripture* but *documents*, *contracts*, *titles*, and, of course, *writing*, that is, a rich composite of power and property, both symbolic and real. Indeed, what Atahualpa fails to recognise, thus precipitating his downfall, is a symbol for an authoritative system of representation and knowledge. Atahualpa, in short, cannot translate from one culture to another.

Like many crepuscular figures, Atahualpa captivates the imagination. School-children in Latin America remember the scene, remember too that Atahualpa made a deal with his captors to fill a room with gold as high as his hand would reach in exchange for his freedom, a deal the Spaniards, needless to say, did not respect. Neruda, in his *Canto general*, memorably amplifies the scene with Pizarro. Borges, in a passing reference to Hernando de Soto, tells us (perhaps apocryphally) that in order to distract Atahualpa during his long imprisonment, it was de Soto who taught the Inca how to play chess. The poignant fantasy built around the Inca prince (to which I myself am right now contributing, to be sure), a fiction bearing little or no relation to the not very sympathetic, historical Atahualpa, is fired by the disproportion between the

---

[1] Garcilaso de la Vega *Historia General del Perú*, vol I (Lima: Librería Internacional del Perú, 1959), p. 74. Translations into English in this chapter are my own unless otherwise stated When quoting from published translations, I have sometimes slightly modified the text for the sake of accuracy.

Inca's trivial gesture and the magnitude of its purported consequences; by the fact that a mere cultural misunderstanding can bring on the loss of a civilisation; by the fact, ultimately, that everything hinges on a book.

I want to stop briefly at another cultural scene, not unrelated to the first one, a scene that has seized the imagination of Mexican historians and novelists alike. The episode, which is also based on contact with the scriptures, does not involve this time the casual rejection of holy writ but, instead, the too vivid, albeit 'deviant', recognition of its letter. Placed in nineteenth-century Chiapas, a district as poor then as it is now, the episode relates how, on a Good Friday, an Indian community, much abused by *mestizo* exploiters, crucify a *mestizo* child, born to a raped Indian mother, in order to measure up to their oppressors. In the Atahualpa legend, destruction resulted from the non-recognition of the book, from its illegibility; in the Chiapas incident – which may be read as a reversal of the first – violence against the oppressors ensues from the book's having been recognised and read too literally. Again, the dramatic situation hinges on a transaction involving a book, signs taken for wonders – or in the case of Atahualpa, not taken for wonders – to use Homi Bhabha's felicitous phrase.[2]

The novelist Rosario Castellanos has fictionalised this scene in her *Oficio de tinieblas*,[3] deliberately transposing it to the 1930s and recycling the episode to make a political statement. Interestingly, research has made it abundantly clear that the 'original' scene itself is apocryphal. Absent from historical records of the period in which it supposedly took place (records that on the other hand did not hesitate to document Indian violence), the scene surfaced as 'fact' in historical writing quite a bit later, when the threat of Indian violence, of which this scene seemed an appropriately gory example, had become a central preoccupation. Manipulated by historians, reappropriated by fiction – one might argue that Castellanos is reading that manipulated history against the grain – this particular scene, as they say, travels well. It is used for shock effect, for example, in the opening shots of the film *The Mission*, where the Guaranís, represented as sweet-tempered, childlike and ultimately deadly, send a crucified friar down the Iguazú falls.

Atahualpa put to death by the Spaniards because he fails to recognise their powerful *escrituras*; the Chiapas indians, according to the way you wish to read the episode, either grotesquely enacting a misreading or empowering themselves through the complex recognition of those very *escrituras*, or doing both at once: these two scenes of reading have points in common, including an immediate dramatic efficacy that I find a little disquieting. One of the sources of that efficacy, I would argue, is the way in which these fictions play into the binary, proposing two distinct and to a point antagonistic cultural spheres, spheres that might be given different names, according to how (and from where) one wishes

---

[2]   Homi Bhabha, 'Signs Taken for Wonders: Questions of Ambivalence and Authority under a Tree Outside Delhi, May 1817', *Critical Inquiry*, vol. 12, no. 1 (1985).
[3]   Rosario Castellanos, *Oficio de tinieblas* (Mexico: Joaquín Martiz, 1962).

to draw one's inevitably ideological lines: names like coloniser and colonised; European and Amerindian; metropolitan and peripheral; civilisation and barbarism; first-world and third-world; West and Non-West; names maybe like *us* and *them*. For the dramatic efficacy of the scene, the spheres need to be kept separate, their oppositional imbalance stressed, and the only negotiation allowed between them must fatefully end in violence, even death.

I will resort now to a third related scene which brings me, finally, to Borges. It is in a story to which I often return, mainly because, though it is staging a similar transaction, it is subtly saying, I think, something different. In 'El Evangelio según Marcos' ['The Gospel According to Mark'],[4] a likeable, conventional young man from Buenos Aires finds himself stranded in a desolate ranch in the pampa. His sole companions are the foreman of the ranch, his son and his daughter – illiterate, barely articulate descendants of Scottish settlers who have intermarried with Indians. Conversation with the three proving impossible, the young man, in order to establish some contact, tries to read to them. First he reads from Ricardo Güiraldes's *Don Segundo Sombra*, a willfully 'nativist', lyrical Argentine novel exalting the hardships of country life and the heroism of country folks. The novel finds scant favour with the Gutres who *are* country folks and don't find country life heroic nor, for that matter, particularly hard. Then Espinosa proceeds to read from an old English family Bible that he comes upon in the house. The blank pages at the end of the volume record the spotty lineage and history of the Guthries, or Gutres, as they are now called, from the time they set forth from Inverness up to the moment when they lost their capacity to read and write. Spurred by vague didactic notions, the young man actually does more than read to them: choosing the Gospel according to Mark, he reads to them: 'para ejercitarse en la traducción y acaso para ver si entendían algo' ['as an exercise in translation, and maybe to find out whether the Gutres understood any of it']. Borges's story is sufficiently ambiguous to leave unclear what is being translated into what. Is it King James's English into twentieth-century Spanish? Is it one cultural system into another? Is it words into life, culture into experience? While we do not know what actual language Espinosa uses to read out loud, we do know that he accompanies his reading with ritual gestures, that he *performs* authority: 'Recordó las clases de elocución en Ramos Mejía y se ponía de pie para predicar las parábolas' ['Remembering his lessons in elocution from his [English]-school days, Espinosa got to his feet when he came to the parables'].

The Gutres turn out to be the most attentive of listeners; in perfect silence they absorb every word and when the Gospel is over demand that it be read to them again 'para entenderlo bien' ['so that they could understand it properly']. The worship they feel for the Book extends to its reader: 'Mientras leía, notó que le retiraban las migas que él había dejado sobre la mesa' ['While he read to

---

[4]   Borges, *Obras completas* (Buenos Aires: Emecé, 1974), pp. 1068-77; 'The Gospel According to Mark', in Emir Rodríguez Monegal and Alistair Reid (eds.), *Borges A Reader* (New York: E.P. Dutton, 1981), pp. 308-11

them, he noticed that they were secretely stealing the crumbs he had dropped on the table']. The end of the story, for all its suddenness, does not come as a surprise. One Friday afternoon, the young man finds himself thinking aloud: 'Ya falta poco' ['It won't be long now']. His words are echoed by the foreman, standing behind him, for his hour is indeed come: he is pushed towards the shed by all three Gutres (the Spanish transliteration of the Scottish surname has a particular ominous, guttural sound to it) and, once inside, beholds the cross they have prepared for him.

Now at first glance this story might seem to illustrate a situation similar to the ones expounded above, that is, the encounter of two distinct and opposed cultures vying for interpretive power, in which one group's 'misreading' results in death for someone from the other. Yet a closer look at the story shows that things are not as simple as they would seem, that cultural binarisms (as if we needed the reminder) are always already compromised, contaminated, always already *mixed*. Borges destabilises both sides, destabilises the encounter's very substance – the negotiation of the book, the act of (reciprocal) misreading itself. In 'The Gospel According to Mark', the 'white' man from the city and the 'indian' peasants are unstable entities. If, on the one hand, the peasants are the city-dweller's 'other', they are 'others' of a particular kind. The Gutres are not the indigenous inhabitants, or the Spanish-Amerindian *mestizos* that have been routinely reified as 'other' in Latin America. Instead, they are the product of Scots 'gone native', a combination of Inverness and the Argentine pampa. On the other hand, if the young medical student from Buenos Aires is the 'other' for the Gutres/Guthries, he too is a rather complex 'other', although he is described, without apparent irony, as 'uno de tantos muchachos porteños' ['one of the common run of young men from Buenos Aires']. Borges gives him an Anglophile free-thinking father, a devout Catholic mother, and a name, Baltazar Espinosa, unerringly pointing to a Sephardic heritage. He also provides him with a bilingual education in an English school and with a set of beliefs, or 'habits of mind', in which cultural dependency coexists with ambivalent attitudes towards autochthony and a vague sense of national pride: 'el país le importaba menos que el riesgo de que en otras partes creyeran que usamos plumas; veneraba a Francia pero menospreciaba a los franceses; tenía en poco a los americanos, pero aprobaba el hecho de que hubiera rascacielos en Buenos Aires' ['Argentina mattered less to him than a fear that in other parts of the world people might think of us as Indians; he worshipped France but despised the French; he thought little of Americans but approved the fact that there were tall buildings, like theirs, in Buenos Aires; he believed the gauchos of the plains to be better riders than those of hill or mountain country'. Highlighting the impossibility of stable subject positions, Borges's story problematises clean-cut divisions, univocal formulations of difference. It also, most importantly, renders the issue of the transmission of the book immensely complex. For whose is the book, anyway? Borges perversely alters the customary scene of colonial mimicry by making a white, Latin American, distantly Jewish, nonbelieving city-dweller parrot that summa of (Western) linguistic and literary perfection, a King James Bible, for the benefit of Scottish-Indian 'others' who cannot read it and yet to whom it 'really' belongs, as part of their patrimony. Espinosa tells himself: 'Lo llevan en la sangre' ['It is in their blood'].

Any reading of this richly significant story by Borges runs the risk of privileging one of the many directions in which it simultaneously and maddeningly takes its reader, and thus reduce its scope. For the story's importance resides in its sheer undecidability, in its interpretive challenge. Beyond the obvious thwarting of binarism, to which all of Borges's work aspires in one form or another, I would like to retain from it, and build upon the notion of permanent movement claimed for this provokingly heterogeneous Latin American cultural scene, the notion that, in this spectacular encounter with *difference*, there is no fixed 'one' from which to postulate, hierarchically, a different 'other.' Here, everyone, so to speak, is 'equally' different, the Gutres *and* Espinosa, and not the Gutres *from* Espinosa or viceversa. In fact, the whole notion of a fixed 'origin' – or, in the prescriptive language often resorted to in order to affirm hegemony, the notion of a 'norm' – is, in this case, moot. The story does not dwell on dependency, or deviance, or even cultural clash: instead, it spurs the reader to contemplate the infinite ramifications of unending, provocative, risky, cultural transactions and exchanges, in which hierarchies, permanently renegotiated, are not made to last. The lesson that Espinosa, much to his chagrin, does not live to learn is that the burden of interpretation is necessarily shared: that one never reads (or translates) *at* someone but *with* someone; that cultural positioning (even cultural identity) is, like reading and translating, a *relation* and not an imposition. Like many of Borges's characters, like Averroes before him, Espinosa is guilty of inattention. For all his good will (the character is described as having 'una casi ilimitada bondad' ['an almost unlimited kindness']. Espinosa, as they say, 'just doesn't get it.' I shall devote the second part of this chapter to examining different aspects of that vexed reception, using Borges both as an example and as a guide to my commentary.

◆ ◆ ◆

In a provocative book entitled *The Cuban Condition*, Gustavo Pérez Firmat defines this 'condition' – and the word *condition* is cannily taken to mean both basic requirement and productive affliction – as a 'translational sensibility', or, more precisely, a *transculturation*.[5] The latter concept is taken from Cuban anthropologist Fernando Ortiz, who coined the term in his seminal *Contrapunteo cubano del tabaco y del azúcar*,[6] in order to stress the unfinished, processual aspect of Cuban culture. Pérez Firmat writes:

> Ortiz makes Cuba's imperfection a distinctive feature of its culture. He is not simply regurgitating the commonplace that, because of the youth

[5]   Gustavo Pérez Firmat, *The Cuban Condition* (Cambridge, New York, Melbourne. Cambridge University Press, 1989).

[6]   Fernando Ortiz, *Contrapunteo cubano del tabaco y del azúcar advertencia de sus contrastes agrarios, económicos, históricos y sociales, su etnografía y su transculturación* (Havana: Consejo Nacional de Cultura, 1963; also Barcelona, 1973; Havana, 1983).

of the Latin-American republics, cultural syntheses have not *yet* taken place. His position, I believe, is closer to that of the Venezuelan philosopher Enrnesto Mayz Vallenilla, who has defined Latin-American culture as indefinite deferral, as a 'no-ser-*siempre*-todavía' [a sort of an 'always-already- not-yet-being']. It is not only that at the time Ortiz was writing Cuba was in a stage of cultural and political ferment, but that this 'stage' is actually a permanent, defining condition. ... (p. 25).

Although Pérez Firmat chooses to limit the notion of transculturation to Cuba, in a gesture that is autobiographical and culture-specific, I believe it can be extended to the rest of Latin America. So of course did Angel Rama,[7] who based much of his cultural analysis of Latin America on that very notion, although adding a teleological dimension to transculturation with which I don't quite agree. Like Pérez Firmat, and clearly like Borges before him, I prefer to maintain the 'always-already-not-yet-being' side of the process, the dispersion and not the promise of resolution. Or, to quote Pérez Firmat once more, I prefer to read Latin American culture not as *fusion* but as *concoction*, 'a non-synthetic mixture of heterogeneous substances' (p. 25). It is in this disruptive transculturation, disruptive in that (like the situation staged in Borges's story) it avoids permanent positioning, chronological determination, and, above all, fixed representations, that one may find the salient trait of Latin American cultures and also, I would argue, the greatest interest of those cultures. And yet it is that very constitutive aspect that, most often, is translated away by first-world readers. Unyielding diversity is hard to manage, especially when it comes from afar. Indeed, how does one translate a 'translational sensibility'?

Critiquing the metropolitan urge to homogenise so-called 'Third-World Literatures' and contain their representations, levelling them with what he calls (in response to Jameson's ill-advised attempt at restitution) 'the rhetoric of Otherness', Aijaz Ahmad reflects on the problematic availability of certain cultural traditions, for example, literatures of the Indian sub-continent written in indigenous languages.[8] These texts may become available directly, through translation, writes Ahmad; more often, however, they arrive indirectly, in critical essays about those texts that offer 'versions and shadows of texts produced in other spaces of the globe'. To these hard-to-get texts, Ahmad opposes Latin American literatures whose 'direct' availability he stresses:

> Literatures of South America and parts of the Caribbean are *directly* available to the metropolitan critic through Spanish and Portuguese, which are after all European languages. *Entire* vocabularies, styles, linguistic sensibilities exist now in English, French, Italian, for translations from these languages. Europeans and American theorists

---

[7]   See Angel Rama, *Transculturación narrativa en América Latina* (Mexico: Siglo Veintiuno Editores, 1982).

[8]   Aijaz Ahmad, '"Third World Literature" and the Nationalist Ideology', *Journal of Arts and Ideas*, New Delhi, vol. 17-18 (1989), pp. 117-35. Frederic Jameson, 'Third World Literature: the Era of Multinational Capitalism', *Social Text*, vol 15 (1986), pp. 65-88

can either read those literary documents *directly*, or in case one is not entirely proficient in Spanish or Portuguese, he/she can nevertheless speak of their literatures with *easy familiarity* because of the *translatibility* of the originals. (p. 127; my emphasis).

I find the notion of 'easy' translatibility problematic here, since it appears based on a familiarity presented in deceptively linguistic terms. As we know only too well in university departments of foreign languages or of comparative literatures, linguistic competence is a highly charged ideological issue and nothing is 'easy.' If Spanish and Portuguese are 'after all' European languages, they may be a little less European than others. And even if they are 'after all' European, I will argue that they are certainly not considered 'First-World' languages. Let me then correct Ahmad's statement, render a little more complicated what he deems so accessible, and say that Latin American texts appear to offer the *illusion* of an easy familiarity, the *illusion* of translatability, and thus create – perversely and, as far as I am concerned, tragically – the *illusion* of cultural competence, not to mention the *illusion* of institutional expertise, usually based on a smattering of texts. An apparently 'easy' translatability which, in the best of cases, is purely linguistic, is further complicated in this case by ideologies of reception that 'choose', as it were, certain vehicles (but not any vehicle) for that translatability, certain representations and texts (but not any representation or text).

I want to make clear that, in speaking of an illusion of cultural competence, I am not measuring lack of quantitative knowledge, nor am I pointing to informational gaps and suggesting that competence can be gauged by erudition. Gaps are the very trademark of cultural exchange: there is nothing wrong *per se* with isolating a text from its context and recontextualising it, i.e. translating it, as an *objet trouvé* of sorts, into another tradition. Much fecund literary grafting has been done this way: a minor Symbolist, Catulle Mendès, read out of context, did more for turn-of-the-century Latin American literature than Mallarmé. Borges himself, in two instances – 'Pierre Menard' and 'Las versiones homéricas' ['Versions of Homer'] – praises ignorance, or at least indifference, as synonymous with freedom from literary superstition. Menard's indifference to *Don Quixote* allows him to rewrite it with relative ease. In the same way, Borges claims that his 'oportuno desconocimiento del griego' ['fortuitous ignorance of Greek'] alows him to enjoy the 'riqueza heterogénea y hasta contradictoria' ['heterogeneous, even contradictory wealth'] of the English translations of the Odyssey. Conversely, the many translations of *Don Quixote* – a text Hispanic writers inevitably consider 'un monumento uniforme' ['an unvarying monument'] (*Obras completas*, p. 240) – fills him with unease.

But isolating a text from its context and recontextualising it through adaptation or translation into another tradition – as Borges has done, for example, with Stevenson or Chesterton – is not the problem here. It is quite another thing to uncouple selected Latin American texts from their particular mode of functioning within their respective Latin American traditions *and then*

reify that miscellany as a coherent corpus 'fully' representative of an 'entire ...
sensibility' called 'Latin America' or even 'Third-World.' (What exactly it
represents, who selects the criteria of representativeness, and from where,
ideologically speaking, is that selection being made, are of course the key
questions that should be asked here.) What is missing of course from these
reductive attempts at reconstructing 'entire ... sensibilities', is the understanding
of culture as *relation*; one ends up here with a fixed corpus but not with modes
of reading. Borges writes: 'El libro no es un ente incomunicado: es una relación,
es un eje de innumerables relaciones. Una literatura difiere de otra, ulterior o
anterior, menos por el texto que por la manera de ser leída: si me fuera otorgado
leer cualquier página actual – ésta, por ejemplo – como la leerán el año dos mil,
yo sabría cómo será la literatura del año dos mil' ['A book is not an isolated
entity — it is a relation, an axis of innumerable relations. One literature differs
from another, either before or after it, not so much because of the text as for the
manner in which it is read. If I were able to read any contemporary page – this
one for example – as it will be read in the year 2000, I would know what
literature will be like in the year 2000'].[9] The experience that Borges proposes
across time should be equally possible across space.

Several years ago Juan Goytisolo, in a melancholy piece in the *New York
Times Book Review*, pondered on the politics of cultural representation in
general, and the reception of Spanish literature in particular. Spain, he said, was
doomed to being a single-faced country, allowed only one image, exotic of
course, that would 'translate well' in the international market and 'represent'
Spanish culture. The image might change according to the passing of time – say
from the French nineteenth-century's *Espagne romantique* to García Lorca's
dreamlike gypsies, to Camilo José Cela's brutal realism – but there was always a
quota: one image. Latin America, in itself a more fluid cultural composite, has
suffered too from similar reductions in first-world readings, less related to
content than to ideologies of reading, to the 'agendas' of the global cultural
marketplace. They are, in fact, prescriptive in nature, asking the text to conform
to reader expectations, like Jean Cassou who, nearly a century ago, regretted that
Rubén Darío had opted for a derivative symbolism instead of writing about 'ce
dont nous revons, sa forêt et sa pampa natales' ['what we [Europeans] dream of,
his native forests and pampas'].[10] The latter request, so clearly reductive of Latin
America to local colour, foreshadows one of the most recalcitrant forms of
reading Latin American literature – a form that has come to signify, as surely as
Carmen Miranda's fruity cornucopias, 'Latin America': I speak, of course, of
magic realism, the story of which has been written elsewhere. It is not my
intention here to retrace the long, tenacious life of this representational mode,
just to underscore the fact that this purportedly non-mediated mode of
representation is a most literary practice, an excrescence of French surrealism

---

[9] Borges, *Obras completas*, p 747; *Other Inquisitions* (Austin. University of Texas Press, 1964),
p. 164.
[10] Sylvia Molloy, *La Diffusion de la littérature hispano-américaine en France au XXe siècle*
(Paris: Presses Universitaires de France, 1972), p. 58.

'transculturated' to Cuba and, by extension, to the rest of Latin America, born on the same operating table on which Lautréamont's umbrella visited with the sewing-machine. One of the many results of Latin America's translational sensibility, it deceptively broadcasts its presumably unique, affectedly non-bookish, marvellously 'real', Latin American nature. First-world readings, however, are known •to take magic realism at face value, prizing it for its 'documentary' merits, and confine its practitioners to the role of native informants, with no recourse left them but ironic complicity – as in the case of Borges's Gutres who, when asked by Espinosa whether they still remembered Indian raids,'le dijeron que sí, pero lo mismo hubieran contestado a una pregunta sobre la ejecución de Carlos Primero' ['told him yes, but they would have given the same answer to a question about the beheading of Charles I'] (*Obras completas*, p. 1069; 'Gospel', p. 309).

The other first-world reading reserved for Latin American literature that I want to consider might be called the universalising mode which, usually, purges texts of signs of the local. This is, of course, the reading reserved to Borges. It is to this mode that I now turn, but first I want to consider briefly certain aspects of Borges's own relation to 'universal', i.e. Western, texts.

In the early essay bearing the somewhat grandiose title of *El tamaño de mi esperanza* [The Extent of My Hope][11] the young Borges invited his compatriots – 'a los hombres que en esta tierra se sienten vivir y morir, no a los que creen que el sol y la luna están en Europa' ['men who believe they will live and die in this land, not those who think the sun and the moon are in Europe'] (*Tamaño*, p. 5) – to a reflection on Argentine literature. After salvaging a few worthy names from the past, he looked to the future of Argentine culture with a famously subversive final recommendation: 'Nuestra famosa incredulidá, no me desanima. El descreimiento, si es intensivo, también es fe y puede ser manantial de obras .... Una incredulidá grandiosa, vehemente, puede ser nuestra hazaña' ['Our famous scepticism does not discourage me. Disbelief, if intense, is also faith and may be a source of creation .... A splendid, vehement disbelief could well be our accomplishment'] (*Tamaño*, p. 10). This disbelief, which Borges put to good use and to which he constantly invites his reader, is particularly stimulating when it comes to his relation with the European archive. Practising cultural allusion in a way, as he himself agrees, quite different from that of Eliot or Joyce, Borges leads the gullible on, accumulating, in a dazzling array, references that first-world readers will easily recognise, and references perhaps not so familiar, but no less recognisable in that, as Barthes would say, they have already been read. But sprinkled in this reassuring list of classics, like so many blemishes on a polished surface, are the *other* references, the many voices this canonical reader does *not* recognise. What is that reader to do with them – or, more aptly, what does that reader do with them? For Borges's text, in truly egalitarian fashion, endows them with the same authority, the same right to speak, as he does the other, more conventional and more easily identifiable

---

[11]   Borges, *El tamaño de mi esperanza* (Buenos Aires: Proa, 1990)

sources of wisdom. I think here not of the remote Scandinavian scholars one has more or less come to expect from Borges but, in a more general way, of other voices quoted by Borges, of the multiple crisscrossing of local bits of texts, identified or alluded to, that make up an Argentine, a Latin American *entonación*. It is against this concrete Latin American background that Borges's tampering with the European archive suddenly takes on full meaning. For Borges not only questions the authority of that archive (even as he relies on it), by quoting from it irreverentially and thus mimicking its very own authoritarian procedures, he also contaminates that archive (as he gives it new life) by inserting it in a new cultural landscape, in the 'outskirts' – *las orillas* – of Latin American literature. To bring up Browning when speaking of Carriego invites readers to a new view of Carriego; but it also, inevitably, invites them to a new view of Browning, an invitation that, unfortunately, often goes unheeded. Borges practises reading, and asks the unfamiliar reader to practise reading, not as confirmation but, to use Lezama Lima's favoured term, as *irradiation*. It is not only the archive that is given a new setting; the reader too is challenged with the perspective of reading from (and in) the non-metropolitan 'outskirts'.

When discussing Borges's relation to the European archive, Sarmiento's utopian project inevitably comes to mind. In manipulating that archive, Sarmiento's purpose was centripetal. He wanted to congregate: to build a literature, a country, his own self. Viewing the Argentine as a void lacking *letras* (as Atahualpa's world lacked *escritura*), Sarmiento, in typical 19th-century postcolonial fashion, endeavoured to fill that void with mixed (and mixed-up) memories of the European archive, practising a poetics of *bricolage*. Borges, I would argue, goes one step further: with a similar admixture, and with a less univocal concept of nationality to uphold, he is centrifugal. His is a poetics of *débris*.

In *Evaristo Carriego*, [12] that early non-biography doubling as a miscellany which already contains all of Borges in a nutshell, there is a piece titled 'Las inscripciones de los carros' ['Horse-Cart Inscriptions']. It had already been published independently two years earlier under a title one wishes Borges had kept: 'Séneca en las orillas' ['Seneca in the Outskirts'].[13] In it, Borges conjures up a sight frequent in the Buenos Aires of the twenties, the horse-drawn cart with an aphorism written on its side. An amateur of these bits of popular wisdom, which he sees as 'esa desinteresada yapa expresiva, sobrepuesta a las visibles expresiones de ... [la] forma' ['gratuitous bits of expressiveness superimposed on the outward manifestations of form'] (*Obras completas*, p. 148; *Evaristo Carriego*, p. 114), Borges shares with the reader a whimsical commentary on their literary effectiveness:

Yo he visto carrito frutero que, además de su presumible nombre, *El preferido del barrio*, afirmaba en dístico satisfecho

[12]   Borges, *Evaristo Carriego*, trans Norman Thomas Di Giovanni (New York Dutton, 1984).
[13]   Borges. 'Séneca en las orillas', *Síntesis*, vol 2, no 19 (1928), pp. 29-32

Yo lo digo y lo sostengo
Que a nadie envidia le tengo

y comentaba la figura de una pareja de bailarines tangueros sin mucha
luz, con la resuelta indicación: *Derecho viejo*. Esa charlatanería de la
brevedad, ese frenesí sentencioso, me recuerda la dicción del célebre
estadista danés Polonio, de *Hamlet*, o la del Polonio natural, Baltazar
Gracián (*Obras completas*, pp. 149-50).

[I have seen a little fruit cart which, besides having the presumptuous
name 'The Neighbourhood Favorite', proclaimed in a smug couplet:

I say this loud and say it bold
I envy no one in the world.

and, under the picture of a couple locked together in a tango, bore the
caption 'straight to the Point'. Such pithy verbosity, such sententious
frenzy, reminds me of the style of the famous Danish statesman
Polonius or of that real-life Polonius, Baltasar Gracián] (*Evaristo*, p.
116).

After weighing the merits and demerits of various examples of this 'epigrafía
de corralón' ['stable-yard epigraphy'] (*Obras completas*, p. 114; *Evaristo*, p.
116), Borges concludes:

Pero el honor, pero la tenebrosa flor de este censo, es la opaca
inscripción *No llora el perdido*, que nos mantuvo escandalosamente
intrigados a Xul Solar y a mí, hechos, sin embargo, a entender los
misterios delicados de Robert Browning, los baladíes de Mallarmé y los
meramente cargosos de Góngora. *No llora el perdido*; le paso ese clavel
retinto al lector (*Obras completas*, pp. 150-1).

[But the crowning glory, the dusky flower of this survey, is the
mystifying inscription 'The Doomed Man Does Not Weep', which kept
Xul-Solar and me disgracefully perplexed, although we were
accustomed to penetrating the delicate mysteries of Robert Browning,
the trite ones of Mallarmé, and the merely heavy-handed ones of
Góngora. 'The Doomed Man Does Not Weep'; I leave this dark
carnation to the reader (*Evaristo*, p. 118).

I bring up Borges's evocation of this busily popular quoting scene as an *ars
poetica* of sorts, a reflection on his hybrid literary practice. These devalued
snippets taken from the local reality of the outer slums, Borges tells us, work
together with the other, prestigious European text (and perhaps even better than
that other text), to revitalise Borges's belief (his incredulous belief) in literature:
'Yo creía descreer de la literatura, y me he dejado aconsejar por la tentación de
reunir estas partículas de ella' ['I once believed I disbelieved in literature, and
now I have let myself be swayed by the temptation to collect these fragments of

literature'] (*Obras completas*, p. 151; *Evaristo*, p. 118). Endowed with the mobility of the carts they identify, these inscriptions are also quotations from a larger, scattered, dynamic text, fragments of what Borges calls 'un criollismo ... conversador del mundo' (*Tamaño*, p. 10), a Latin American conversation with the world, in which body and letter intersect:

> Son ademanes perdurados por la escritura, son una afirmación incesante. Su alusividad es la del conversador orillero que no puede ser directo narrador o razonador y que se complace en discontinuidades, en generalidades, en fintas: sinuosas como el corte (*Obras completas*, p. 150).

> [They are gestures captured in writing, a ceaseless affirmation .... Their allusiveness is that of the outer-slums dweller who cannot tell a story plainly or logically but delights in meaningful gaps, in generalizations, and in sidesteps that are as sinuous as a fancy tango figure] (*Evaristo*, p. 118).

A horse-drawn cart loaded with references and allusions (both to the European text and to the neighbourhood book of wisdom), carrying a text that unravels as the cart wends its way though the outskirts (for these carts routinely shun the centre of the city) – this is a rather apt figuration, as pleasing to the eye as it is promising to the mind, of a practice of literature that weaves the European text together with local *dicta* and gestures, postulating that *almost the same, but not quite* that is, for Homi Bhabha, the hallmark of colonial mimicry.[14] Yet this is the very practice of literature whose complexities and contradictions, whose ambivalence, are routinely ironed out by first-world readers, the very ones that profess to 'understand' Borges. The Universal (in its European, Western avatar) lays claim on Borges and the practice of literature he stands for, but does so against the grain, failing to recognise – perhaps because Borges's text 'passes' so easily – its double-voicedness, its fundamentally mobile, relational nature. Beatriz Sarlo, not so long ago, spoke of the uncanniness of lecturing in England on a writer whose first-world reputation had 'cleansed him of nationality'.[15] I was reminded of the similar, drastic cleansing undergone by Borges when first translated into French. 'Let us not look for the "Argentine writer" in him', one critic wrote. 'Although he loves and often speaks of his country, Borges is not representative of Argentine literature, he is a monster and a genius' (Molloy, *La Diffusion*, p. 219). Another French critic put it more bluntly, 'he belongs more to Europe than to Latin America' (Molloy, *La Diffusion*, p. 208).

Borges, who splendidly represents the 'translational sensibility' described by Pérez Firmat, or the 'transcultural Westernism' of Latin America, as George

---

[14] Homi K. Bhabha, 'Of Mimicry and Man: The Ambivalence of Colonial Discourse', in Bhabha, *The Location of Culture* (London and New York. Routledge, 1994), pp. 85-92.
[15] Beatriz Sarlo, *Jorge Luis Borges A Writer on the Edge* (London· Verso, 1993)

Yúdice has called it,[16] is domesticated, classified, ironically victimised by the binary, the *either/or* he has fought, on aesthetic and ideological terms, throughout his life.

There is another passage in Borges that sums up this vexed reception admirably in my view:

> En el siglo VI, una sirena fue capturada y bautizada en el norte de Gales ... Otra, en 1403, pasó por una brecha en un dique, y habitó en Harlem hasta el día de su muerte. Nadie la comprendía, pero le enseñaron a hilar.... Un cronista del siglo XVI razonó que no era un pescado porque sabía hilar, y que no era una mujer porque podía vivir en el agua (*Discusión*, p. 85).

> [In the 6th century, a siren was captured and baptised in northern Wales ... In 1403, another siren slipped through a hole in a dam and lived in Haarlem till the day she died. No one understood her but they taught her how to spin ... A sixtenth-century chronicler reasoned that she was not a fish because she knew how to spin and that she was not a woman because she could live in the water.]

Borges's *difference* – his hybridity – like that of the mermaid's, cannot be easily read. It is no less there, like hers, in that irresolvable, ever-fruitful in-between.

---

[16]   George Yúdice, 'We Are Not the World', *Social Text* (1992), pp 202-16.

CHAPTER 2

How European is it?

William Rowe

Un hombre puede ser enemigo de otros hombres [. . .]
pero no de un país (Jorge Luis Borges)

A man can be the enemy of other men [. . .] but not of a country

El éxstasis no repite sus símbolos (Jorge Luis Borges)

Ecstasy does not repeat its symbols[1]

Frontiers

I begin with a piece of writing from 1924:

> The Rhine is still the Rhine, the great divider. You feel it as you cross.
> The flat, frozen, watery places. Then the cold and curving river. Then
> the other side, seeming so cold, so empty, so frozen, so forsaken. The
> train stands and steams fiercely. Then it draws through the flat Rhine
> plain, past frozen pools of flood-water, and frozen fields, in the
> emptiness of this bit of occupied territory.
>
> Immediately you are over the Rhine, the spirit of place has changed.
> There is no more attempt at the bluff of geniality. The marshy places
> are frozen. The fields are vacant. There seems nobody in the world.
>
> It is as if the life had retreated eastwards. As if the Germanic life were slowly
ebbing away from contact with western Europe, ebbing to the deserts of the
east.[2]

This is part of 'A Letter from Germany', written by D.H. Lawrence in 1924
and published posthumously in 1934. To read it in the late 1990s, from inside
the current boundaries of the European Community, is to be made aware of how
the frontier between inside and outside has moved eastwards and southwards.
What is called 'European' has expanded – however one draws the boundary –
but if Europe is the EC it is becoming increasingly difficult for people from

---

[1] All translations are mine, except where indicated
[2] D H Lawrence, *A Selection from Phoenix* (Harmondsworth: Penguin 1979), pp. 116-7

outside to get in. All immigration is now subject to a single computer archive. Europe has been and is a concern with frontiers, keeping those who are not 'ready' – formerly the 'barbarians', to use one word for many – outside. But is the EC Europe? Where – an old topic for lapidary phrases – does Europe end? How European is it? And what happens if one were to read Lawrence's haunting statement from the work of Borges?

Let me be clear: that would not mean reading an English writer through an Argentinian one. The boundaries called up in the words *English* and *Argentinian* would spoil the pleasure of reading, one form of which is Borges's anarchic utopia in which all books are imagined as written by a single author – a complete deterritorialisation of reading. Those adjectives, *English* and *Argentinian*, make a territory national and a nation territorial, and their literatures an expression of those fantastic wholes. Literary nationalism has the ground taken from under it in Borges's essay 'El escritor argentino y la tradición' or in the place called Tlön (in the story 'Tlön, Uqbar, Orbis Tertius') whose literature has no nouns – and therefore no territorial adjectives derived from them.[3] Placing Borges alongside Lawrence helps to reveal how radical Borges's handling of frontiers is.

To read across frontiers, which in different ways is the invitation of all of the *Ficciones* stories, includes doubting whether everything inside a country can be an expression of it:

Pensé que un hombre puede ser enemigo de otros hombres, de otros momentos de otros hombres, pero no de un país: no de luciérnagas, palabras, jardines, cursos de agua, ponientes (*Ficciones*, p. 103).[4]

I thought that a man can be the enemy of other men, of other moments of other men, but not of a country: not of fireflies, words, gardens, streams, sunsets.

The thought belongs to Yu Tsun, who, in 'The Garden of Forking Paths', is a Chinese, spying for the Germans against the British in the First World War. Most of the stories in *Ficciones* were written during the Second World War, a time of exacerbation of frontiers and bloodshed for territory. But how inescapable is that lining up of territory, culture and language as identity – of nation and state as Fatherland? For the present, I would like to suggest that those concentric symmetries depend on a particular unification of time. Later, I will point to how the materials of *Ficciones* include the formation of the Argentinian state, in the nineteenth and twentieth centuries. But for the moment I want to return to the question: what happens if one reads the terms of European frontier-

---

[3]   In more detail, the literature of northern Tlön has verbs in place of nouns and that of the south, monosyllabic adjectives. If the latter 'correspond to a real object it is by mere chance'. (*Ficciones*, p. 21)

[4]   *Ficciones* (Buenos Aires Emecé, 1956), *El aleph* (Barcelona Seix Barral, 1983)

making from Borges's work?

Residue or sacrifice

Yu Tsun's narrative – and Borges's text, whose title, 'The Garden of Forking Paths', is also the title of the first half of *Ficciones* – ends with an incompatibility: the Chinaman has managed to send a message to his German chief (Viktor Runeberg, a name that piles up victory / sacred signs / mountain in different combinations of nouns and adjectives) by sacrificing a human being for his name:

> El Jefe ... sabe que mi problema era indicar ... la ciudad que se llama Albert y que no hallé otro medio que matar a una persona de ese nombre (*Ficciones*, p. 111).

> The Chief ... knows my problem was to indicate ... the city called Albert, and that I found no other means to do so than to kill a man of that name.

But his final statement is: 'No sabe (nadie puede saber) mi innumerable contrición y cansancio' (*Ficciones*, p. 111) ['He does not know (no one can know) my innumerable contrition and weariness']. The innumerable, the unnarratable: how to reconcile this with the success of the secret message? Contrition and weariness become the latter's residue.

It is possible to read the incompatibility of message and residue as a subject for Literary Theory, which would amount to putting a particular boundary on how the story is to be read. But what happens if one reads this story from other Borges stories? Say from 'The God's Writing', in the collection *El aleph*, much of which was also written during the Second World War. The narrator is a Mayan priest, held in captivity by a pyramid-burning Spanish conquistador. The priest's concern is to discover a magic statement ('una sentencia mágica') written by the native god on the first day of creation, because this statement is capable of undoing present misfortune ('apta para conjurar esos males'). He does not know where the god's statement is to be found or what material and what signs it is made of (a mountain might be the god's word), but it occurs to him that if a voice or word ('voz') is articulated by a god, it cannot be 'inferior al universo o menos que la suma del tiempo' (*El aleph*, p. 119) ['inferior to the universe or less than the sum of time']. Which actually makes it a message without a residue, that is, the Word. At that point he becomes dizzy ('me infundió una especie de vértigo').

He then experiences – that is, the text produces – two configurations: the first suffocating, the second releasing. The first is a succession of infinitely concentric dreams. The endless circles inside each other – configuring the desire for, or addiction to, totality that the word 'universe' conjures – he discovers to be worse than the prison of stone he is confined in. The second offers a different type of space-time, bordered but infinitely expansive:

> Yo vi una Rueda altísima, que no estaba delante de mis ojos, ni detrás, ni a los lados, sino en todas partes, a un tiempo. Esa Rueda estaba hecha de agua, pero también de fuego, y era (aunque se veía el borde) infinita. Entretejidas, la formaban todas las cosas que serán, que son y que fueron (*El aleph*, p. 121).

> I saw an exceedingly high Wheel, which was not before my eyes, nor behind me, nor to the sides, but in every place at one time. That Wheel was made of water, but also of fire, and it was (though its edge could be seen) infinite. Interwoven, all things that are, were and shall be formed it.

The ability to understand everything ('entendiéndolo todo') makes him capable also of understanding the god's writing. But, at this point or threshold, he decides not to use the fourteen-word formula.

> Quien ha entrevisto el universo, quien ha entrevisto los ardientes designios del universo, no puede pensar en un hombre, en sus triviales dichas o desventuras, aunque ese hombre sea él. Ese hombre *ha sido él* y ahora no le importa. Qué le importa la suerte de aquel otro, qué le importa la nación de aquel otro, si él, ahora es nadie (*El aleph*, p. 121).

> Whoever has seen the universe, whoever has beheld the fiery design of the universe, cannot think in terms of one man, of that man's trivial fortunes or misfortunes, though he be that very man. That man *has been he* and now matters no more to him. What is the life of that other to him, the nation of that other to him, if he, now, is no one?

The priest has been split into two men: the one who is now nobody, without nation or identity, and doesn't care about those things, and the other who has been subsumed into a totalitarian scheme, in other words, has been sacrificed. The first man, the one who now speaks, has become a mere residue to the splendour he has seen. The god's writing, for its part, is precisely a message without a residue, a language that leaves nothing out, like the language of angels, who, as Borges writes, 'speak through intelligible species, that is through direct representations and without any verbal mystery'.[5] A language without leakage or ambiguities is the property of transcendent beings – or the desire of human beings who claim to be the agents of some transcendent principle that demands sacrifice from other people – the most notorious twentieth-century example being the idea of bloodshed and sacrifice (of Jews, gypsies, homosexuals ...) in order to make Europe 'whole'. Less openly, such a language,

---

[5]   Borges, 'Indagación de la palabra', in *El idioma de los argentinos* (Buenos Aires: Gleizer Editores, 1928).

and the power it conjures, expresses the desires of bureaucratic control.

Rather than that, the man (not a priest any more) in Borges's story prefers to be a residue. That way he sees things as unlimited multiplicities: which is what writing is – not the god's but Borges's. The working of Borges's writing, with its exposure of that desire for totality, may be contrasted with Protestant justification and Hegelian dialectic, which are both revealed as particularly German forms of sacrificial thinking in the story 'Deutsches requiem', whose protagonist writes 'Nadie puede ser ... nadie puede probar una copa de agua o partir un trozo de pan, sin justificación' (El aleph, p. 84) ['No-one can exist ... no-one can put a glass of water to his mouth or break a piece of bread, without justificacion.'][6] But, to quote Walter Abisch's title, 'How German is it'?[7]

Interstices or encirclement

The Maya priest's visionary wheel – a multiple space available as simultaneity – resembles the Aleph in the story of that name (dated 1943). The Aleph cannot be narrated: the 'unresolvable' problem is 'la enumeración siquiera parcial, de un conjunto infinito' (El aleph, p. 167) ['the enumeration, albeit partial, of an infinite set']. All that can be done is to 'transcribe' it partially ('algo'). But this is precisely what its owner – a spectacularly bad poet in Buenos Aires – has been doing, in order to write a turgid epic poem. The poet in question is called Carlos Argentino Daneri: once again the territorial adjective, here as Christian name; the state baptising its sons with appropriately prestigious inheritances (the Argentinian Dante or Charles Darwin, the latter become, after the age of thirty, in his own words, 'a kind of machine for grinding general laws out of large collections of facts' and incapable of reading 'a line of poetry').[8]

But the Aleph, endlessly multiple, is incompatible with the epic story of the nation as a timeless splendour. It institutes an anti-epic time, a time with endless residues, like William Empson's 'missing dates' in the poem of that title, written in the 1930s, whose repeated chorus runs 'The waste remains, the waste remains and kills' – no immortality there! In 'The Garden of Forking Paths', any potential for epic narrative offered by events of the First World War is undone by their porousness to multiple interstices. The story is framed as a gloss on page 22 of Liddell Hart's standard History of the War, but the frame is exceeded by the gloss – the diegesis makes a residue that is incommensurable with history. The sub-plot (Yu Tsun's machinations) not only introduces into the plot an interstice that becomes an abyss, a hole which cannot be closed; it also includes a further – redundant – sub-plot which is an endlessly bifurcating novel. Such an

---

[6] The epigraph to 'Deutsches requiem' is a quotation from the book of Job and the story may be taken, as A Dictionary of Borges suggests, as dramatising a German reading of a Jewish text. (E. Fishburn and P Hughes, A Dictionary of Borges (London· Duckworth, 1990), pp 125-6)

[7] Walter Abisch, How German Is It? (New York· New Directions, 1980)

[8] Charles Darwin, The Autobiography of Charles Darwin, 1809-1892 (London: Collins, 1958), p 139.

arrangement is inadmissible in historiography, where time is an explanatory, or at least accumulative, process. In that Chinese novel,[9] every event has several outcomes: enemies become friends and vice versa, the lines cannot be drawn and human beings, objects and territories still less, therefore, lined up. The sequence of sub-plots, each inside its predecessor, is potentially endless; topologically, each successive inside becomes an outside, turning the Mayan priest's concentric circles inside out and making a machine that works in an opposite way to Darwin's, in that it permits no general laws.

The unlimited bifurcations may be taken as a modelling of time: the bifurcating novel of the sub-sub plot, whose title is the title of the whole text, is 'un invisible laberinto de tiempo' (*Ficciones*, p. 1050 ['an invisible labyrinth of time']. This is not the absolute, uniform time of Newton, or of the Universal History proposed by the Enlightenment or positivism, models for the histories of the new nations of emancipated Latin America. Its proximity produces a particular sensation in Yu Tsun:

> Sentí a mi alrededor y en mi oscuro cuerpo una invisible, intangible pululación. No la pululación de los divergentes, paralelos y finalmente coalescentes ejércitos, sino una agitación más inaccesible, más íntima y que ellos de algún modo prefiguraban (*Ficciones*, p. 108).

> I felt about me and in my dark body an invisible, intangible swarming. Not the swarming of the divergent, parallel and finally coalescent armies [the Chinese novel describes the movements of Chinese armies], but a more inaccessible, more intimate agitation that they in some manner prefigured.

The term 'pululación' could equally well be translated as 'spawning'. The Spanish Academy's *Diccionario Manual* gives as definitions 'empezar a brotar ... vástagos un vegetal; abundar, multiplicarse en un paraje los insectos y sabandijas'. The references to vegetation and insects introduce a somewhat less human, or less mammalian, implication than Corominas's derivation of 'pulular' from the Latin *pullus* = 'cría de animal' giving the meaning 'aparecer en abundancia'.[10]

Yu Tsun's narrative continues:

> Volví a sentir esa pululación ... Me pareció que el húmedo jardín que rodeaba la casa estaba saturado hasta lo infinito de invisibles personas (*Ficciones*, p. 110).

---

[9]   No more or no less Chinese than the 'Chinese encyclopedia', which Foucault quotes at the beginning of *The Order of Things* to exemplify an unstable episteme, and which could also be read as a Latin American episteme. (Michael Foucault, *The Order of Things An Archaeology of the Human Sciences*, London: Tavistock Publications, 1970).

[10]   Joan Corominas, *Breve diccionario etimológico de la lengua castellana* (Madrid Gredos, 1961), p 456

Once again I felt the swarming sensation of which I have spoken ... It seemed to me that the humid garden that surrounded the house was infinitely saturated with invisible persons.

This teeming or seething is, because of its infinity of dimensions, not just incompatible with history – with grand narratives, or even with any accumulation in time – but ultimately with any narrative: the text ends, a few sentences further on, with the innumerable.

The final paragraph speaks of the residue: of what is left over after the Chinaman has succeeded in sending his message – in adding his invisible sentence, his redundant writing to the History of the War. 'Lo demás es irreal, insignificante' (*Ficciones*, p. 111) ['the rest is unreal, insignificant'], he declares, and finally speaks of his 'inumerable contrición y cansancio' ['innumerable contrition and weariness']. As last words, these recall (Shakespeare's) Hamlet's. If taken as a model of reading, the text displays a huge porosity to European literature. It approximates to Borges's ideal horizon of reading all books as if written by a single author. There are various ways of considering this aspect of Borges's writing. The one most commonly discussed is intertextuality. I prefer to suggest another one: the fact that this complexity of association implies particular memory structures.

Crucial in all this is how form and material, signs and their material supports, continually change places, which is to run against one of the central lines of continental European thought, hylomorphism,[11] and to move into unlimited empiricism.[12] For example, the sub-plots of 'The Garden of Forking Paths' can be taken as form or information: as formal interpolations of narrative sequences or as interpolations in the sense of an archive of glosses, but glosses which in turn become interstices in the formal organisation of the story. As bifurcations they make nonsense of any *relato de identidad* (story of identity), just as porosity undermines the physical frontiers that defend national territories.[13]

The huge range of textual echoes can be read as erudition, as an example of T. S. Eliot's idea of tradition (the whole of European literature since Homer), that is, a stable inheritance, as in the Classical idea of a fixed stack of *topoi*, which add up to an organised space or fixed spatialisation of memory. 'The

---

[11] See A N Whitehead, *Process and Reality* (New York Free Press, 1979), pp 49-50: 'All modern philosophy hinges round the difficulty of describing the world in terms of subject and predicate, substance and quality, particular and universal. The result always does violence to that immediate experience which we express in our actions, our hopes, our sympathies, our purposes, and which we enjoy in spite of our lack of phrases for its verbal analysis We find ourselves in a buzzing world, amid a democracy of fellow creatures: whereas, under some disguise or other, orthodox philosophy can only introduce us to solitary substances, each enjoying an illusory experience '

[12] See Gilles Deleuze, *Dialogues* (London· Athlone Press, 1987) and Borges's use (in 'New Refutation of Time') of Locke and Hume on time the deterritorialisations of early (British) capitalism

[13] See David Viñas, *Indios, ejército y frontera* (Mexico City, 1984), p 90.

Library of Babel' offers an explosive parody of such an attitude: the stacked cells that the librarians live inside of only *seem* to guarantee the order (authority) the institution promises. And Borges's parodic handling of the fixity inherent in the notion of Archive is well known. A prime example is the so-called 'Chinese encyclopedia', mentioned above, which appears in the *Manual de zoología fantástica* [*Manual of Fantastic Zoology*] (as well as in 'John Wilkins's Analytic language'). There is also the remark Borges made in a lecture, that 'it would be fair to say that Western culture is not pure in the sense that it is only partially Western' ('cabría decir que la cultura occidental es impura en el sentido de que sólo es a medias occidental').[14]

The state, monuments and chaos

How and where does the anarchic instability arise? If the material of the interpolations or bifurcations consists mainly in texts written in Europe (even the Chinese armies have come via there), their form – in this story once again there is a 'pululación' or swarming effect – is time. But time is not formal but material. Time enters Borges's texts not as the uniformly measured mathematical time of Newton but as the innumerable time of John Locke[15] – or of Ireneo Funes, one of the most interesting actions of the story 'Funes the Memorious' being the way in which it unleashes inside the art of memory the incessant movement of time: an invaded or invasive archive.

'Funes the Memorious', dated 1942, locates the story it tells in the 1880s. Funes the character's brief life spans 1868 to 1889. Described as a Uruguayan with characteristics of the 'orillero antiguo' (old-time inhabitant of the suburbs), the first feature which takes him out of the ordinary – which individuates – is his sense of absolute time: he knows the time to the minute, 'sin consultar el cielo' (*Ficciones*, p. 118) ['without consulting the sky'] – no gaucho he! The final image given is that of Funes's face at dawn, aged 19: 'me pareció monumental, como el bronce, más antiguo que Egipto, anterior a las profecías y a las pirámides' (*Ficciones*, p. 127) ['he seemed to me monumental as bronze, more ancient than Egypt, older than the prophecies and the pyramids'].

That statement, which in an immediate sense belongs to the narrator of the story, includes several voices, one of them that of the biographer as maker of public monuments. Where is that voice coming from? What society, what enunciative field makes it possible? Because apart from the Romantic style –

---

[14] Jorge Luis Borges, *Siete noches* (Mexico City Fondo de Cultura Económica, 1980), p. 62.

[15] Locke writes of time as 'perpetually perishing' (see Whitehead, *Process and Reality*, p. 210). This idea is implicit in Borges's 'New Refutation of Time'. Fishburn and Hughes state that 'most of the intellectual argument of "Funes the Memorious" stems from Locke's discussion of language in book 3, ch 1 of the *Essay* [*Concerning Human Understanding*], in which he considers the relationship of language and things, noting that whereas "all Things are Particulars, the far greatest part of Words that make all Languages are General Terms"' (*A Dictionary of Borges*, p. 143). Locke's statement includes the possibility of unlimited empiricism.

appropriate to the 1880s in that that period may be taken, in terms of literary history, as a fulfillment in positivist monumentality of Sarmiento's romantic epic – there are specific issues about the field it emerges from and speaks of ('between the lines').

The 1880s are a key decade in the consolidation of the modern Argentinian state. Technological modernisation (centred on beef and railways) and rationalisation of the public sphere, converged with a new politics and logistics of territory: the Conquest of the Desert, against the Indians to the South, conducted through new high-speed technologies (electric telegraph and Remington repeater rifle), had been accomplished by General Julio Argentino Roca, who became president in 1880. The old, rural Argentina became, increasingly, a memory. The old, porous, frontier became a logistical and ideological wall.[16] The state was now able to give material fulfilment to that discourse of monumentality which it was supposed to embody.

The connections between industrial technology as discipline or training and the internalisation of clock time are well known: Funes does not consult the sky, marker of preindustrial time as opposed to what, in Britain, used to be called railway time because the uniform time of rail timetables did not coincide with the time of sundials. Less easy to document are the alterations in the modes of memory storage, though the general sense is clear: a shift towards writing and reading as both site and modelling of memory.[17] Funes, who learns Latin by reading Pliny's *Natural History*, exists between two epochs or in both at once: if Pliny's chaotic collection of data represents a 'pre'-modern episteme, Funes's perception of time – as a single and absolute series dependent on clocks – is modern. Yet the epochally disparate attributes of his mentality cannot be read homogeneously, since they model the act of reading differently and speak of different types of mental training: on the one hand the archaic and non-classified and on the other the modern, classified and tabulated; the one can be read from the other, in either direction.

Of course, the label 'mentality' applied to Funes is problematic, because it depends on his being the subject of a biography, and biography sculpts an identity which is incommensurable with micro perception. The incommensurabilities of the story can be taken as a collision of epochs (archaic and modern) and of spaces (urban and rural). Yet to organise one's reading in this particular way is to organise it sociologically, that is along precisely those lines of rational organisation which were made possible by modernity: it is precisely such acts of classification that become untenable if read from Funes's 'mind'. Because it is not just that Funes's perceptions are chaotic, they are also perfectly ordered:

---

[16]   See Viñas, *Indios, ejército y frontera*
[17]   See Jack Goody, *The Domestication of the Savage Mind* (Cambridge: Cambridge University Press, 1977).

Nosotros, de un vistazo, percibimos tres copas en una mesa; Funes, todos los vástagos y racimos y frutos que comprende una parra. Sabía las formas de las nubes australes del amanecer del treinta de abril de mil ochocientos ochenta y dos y podía compararlas en el recuerdo con las vetas de un libro en pasta española que había mirado una vez y con las líneas de la espuma que un remo levantó en el Río Negro en la acción del Quebracho (*Ficciones*, p. 123).

We, in one glance, can perceive three cups on a table; Funes, all the leaves and tendrils and fruit that make up a vine. He knew the forms of the southern clouds at dawn on the thirtieth of April eighteen eighty two and he could compare them in his memory with the whirls on a book bound in Spanish leather that he had looked at once and with the lines of foam raised by an oar in the Rio Negro during the battle of Quebracho.

The battle referred to was, in the words of a note in an English edition of *Ficciones*, 'a landmark in Uruguayan history'.[18] Yet what are vast constructs such as 'Uruguay' and 'history' beside Funes's perceptions? The infinity of particulars would make them untenable; they are the province of the narrator, who introduces a number of references to the establishment of Uruguay as an independent territory. In this sense, the text produces an emergence of chaos inside those large orders of space and time. But it is not just a question of chaos arising inside order; order also emerges inside chaos, in that everything, for Funes, is capable of becoming a form. Funes's perceptions can be read in two directions which cannot be synthesised: everything becomes form / all forms dissolve. Chaos arises inside order and order inside chaos, endlessly, as in chaos theory, or as in Heraclitan fire or Dionysian ecstasy.[19] Why do critics tend to ignore this dimension of Borges's writing? This happens, I suggest, because literary criticism tends to work from inherited assumptions about the stability of texts, assumptions which depend upon the stabilities provided by institutions.

This therefore is a text that offers not just a historicisation of the act of reading but a radical disturbance of it, that is a disturbance of the training which has taught one to extract recognisable patterns. It proposes a poetics that cannot be contained inside a sociology of knowledge. Writing/reading is placed at a threshold of emergence, just as Mallarmé in his epochal poem 'Un coup de dés', invented ways of thinking 'le hazard', in other words of producing becoming,

---

[18]   G Brotherston and P Hulme, *J L Borges, Ficciones* (London: Harrap, 1976), p. 176. See also Fishburn and Hughes, *A Dictionary of Borges*, p 198, for a less monumental account.

[19]   See J. Cohen and J. Stewart, *The Collapse of Chaos* (London: Viking, 1994), chapter 1, especially p 20. Heraclitus 'el cosmos . ha sido, es y será un fuego vivo, incesante, que se enciende y se apaga sin desmesura' – used by J.J. Saer as an epigraph (see below) (fragment 30: 'The ordering [kosmos], the same for all, no god nor man has made, but it ever was and is and will be: fire everliving, kindled in measures and in measures going out'; C. Kahn, *The Art and Thought of Heraclitus* (Cambridge. Cambridge University Press, 1979, p. 132). Dionysos: see Gilles Deleuze, *Nietzsche and Philosophy* (London Athlone Press, 1983), especially chapter 1, sections 5-7, and chapter 2, section 5

without recourse to gods, including the 'mortall god' of the state and its bureaucratic organisation. Where Mallarmé uses an imagery of shipwreck, that is, of the collapse of the most advanced technology of the time (1897), Borges stages a shipwreck of European knowledge and of the Latin American invention of nations.

Funes sees everything minutely:

> Refiere Swift que el emperador de Lilliput discernía el movimiento del minutero; Funes discernía contínuamente los tranquilos avances de la corrupción, de las caries, de la fatiga (*Ficciones*, pp. 125-6).

> Swift relates that the emperor of Lilliput could discern the movement of the minute hand; Funes could continuously discern the tranquil advance of corruption, of decay, of fatigue.

That capacity implies, in the social use of technology, the possibility of total surveillance via total registration (writing), something only the state as bureaucratic machine that produces classification, archives, files, can promise. But Funes's capability also displays the impossibility of total storage: he remembers everything but it takes him a day to assemble the memories of a previous day. The problem is time. Or, more precisely, time-space.

There are different ways of responding to this problem – different places it can be read from. But before considering these I would like to mention a related issue.

Reading machine/Hole machine

European culture enters the text of 'Funes' through a multitude of references, some named and some not. They include – to mention just a few – Plato, Kant, early church history, Locke, Pliny, Linnaeus and Swift. But *reference* is not an adequate term. Because Borges's text is over-glossed – over-determined – in a kind of unboundaried heteroglossia. In other words, there is here the proposal of an endlessly porous operation of reading. That porousness does not, however, entail passivity. The text is a reading machine, that produces readings of other texts, readings of other readings, including itself.

How does the machine work? Better, what is the work it does? Funes's world – in fact the wrong word because sensations, perceptions and memories are the same for him so that there is not yet a world, or what Wittgenstein, in the first sentence of the *Tractatus*, calls 'the case' for him. But, if 'world' is used as shorthand, Funes's world is innumerable – and this is the case whether numbers are taken as signs or as underlying ratios. The reading actions that the text displays occur at a particular intersection: between the innumerable and the archive (most, though by no means all of which is European). The term 'cultural code', used by Roland Barthes in *S/Z*, is not appropriate to the memory-stores of written texts that are implicated, because the effect of the intersection between the archive and the innumerable is not a codification but an instability.

According to Beatriz Sarlo,

> 'Funes the Memorious' can be understood as a fictional mise-en-scène of the enslavement of a discourse by direct experience. Funes has an infinite memory but is incapable, Borges asserts, of thinking: 'To think is to forget differences, generalise, make abstractions. In the teeming world of Funes, there were only details, almost immediate in their presence.'[20] Literature is precisely (and specifically), a symbolic practice that breaks with the immediacy of memory, perception and repetition. Literature works with the heterogeneous, it cuts, pastes, skips over things, mixes: operations which Funes cannot carry out with his perceptions, nor, as a result, with his memories.[21]

But from where, and according to what organising principles does literature carry out its cutting, pasting and skipping over? Sarlo associates Funes, as 'doomed to remain in thrall to the material of his experience', with Argentina as 'peripheral' to the 'centre', which is the 'advanced' countries that dominate in the production of wealth and knowledge. The implication seems to be that Argentina – unlike Europe – only becomes readable from the outside, Funes representing the River Plate area without literature.

This can be checked with an experiment. The idea would be to test what happens when 'Funes' is read alongside two texts of which it is the 'precursor' in Borges's sense of that word – that is, texts that select it – one by Juan José Saer (born in 1937 in the Province of Santa Fe, north of Buenos Aires) and the other by Paul Celan (Romania 1920 – Paris 1970). In Saer's novel, *Nadie nada nunca* (1980), whose events occur during the recent military dictatorship, a character referred to as 'el Bañero' enters a process similar to Funes's:

> su universo conocido perdía cohesión, pulverizándose, transformándose en un torbellino de corpúsculos sin forma, y tal vez sin fondo, donde ya no era tan fácil buscar un punto en el cual hacer pie ...[22]

> una muchedumbre de imágenes, de latidos, de pulsaciones lo atraviesan, contínuos, como una piedra que cuando se la da vuelta deja ver el grumo efervescente de un hormiguero.[23]

> his known universe lost coherence, became pulverised, turning into a

---

[20]   The translation is from *Labyrinths* (Harmondsworth· Penguin, 1970) p. 94.
[21]   B Sarlo, *Jorge Luis Borges, A Writer on the Edge* (London· Verso, 1993), p 30.
[22]   Juan José Saer, *Nadie nada nunca* (Mexico Siglo XXI, 1980), p 117
[23]   Saer, *Nadie nada nunca*, p 126

whirlwind of corpuscles without form, and perhaps without background, where it was no longer easy to find a place to stand ...

a multitude of images, vibrations, pulsations pass through him, continuous, like a stone that when turned over reveals the effervescent mass of an anthill.

One of the most interesting things in Saer's novel, which uses Heraclitus's Fragment 30 as an epigraph, is the effect of reading these passages upon one's sense of time, and of that on what is taken to be history (specifically upon the history of 'el proceso', the period of military rule in Argentina). Reading them can also put a different inflection upon Sarlo's assumption that 'Funes' is 'a *conte philosophique* on literary theory [which] can be understood as a parable dealing with the possibilities and impossibilities of representation'; 'a hyperbolic image of the devastating effects of an absolute and naive realism which trusts the "natural" force of perceptions and events'.[24] Because read from Saer, Funes's 'world' emerges clearly as a dramatisation of pure becoming, the becoming that precedes 'experience' and that needs to be stabilised before historiography can organise time. And, with its mentions of the history of the foundation of Uruguay as nation-state, the text can be read as a machine that makes holes in the imaginary unity of that history. Or, perhaps more accurately, 'Funes' can be read as displaying a reading action that makes holes in the making of that nation-state, and by implication, of that other one called Argentina. And the interstices occurring in that way of reading arise not just beween entities (Argentina / Europe, country / city, etc.) but inside entities. This is where the apparent paradox of a space that is bordered but expansive becomes particularly interesting. A space that has borders but the multiple inside it sloughs off any single definition (or predication) like 'English' or 'Argentinian' of 'Chinese' or 'German'. Deterritorialisation does not mean having no borders.

Once one starts to read 'Funes the Memorious' non-allegorically, Funes the character begins to resemble what Borges in 1952 said about Macedonio Fernández at the latter's graveside:

Filósofo es, entre nosotros, el hombre versado en la historia de la filosofía, en la cronología de los debates y en las bifurcaciones de las escuelas. ... A Macedonio, en cambio ... las circunstancias y las fechas de la filosofía no le importaron, pero sí la filosofía.[25]

A philosopher, among us [between ourselves], is the man who is versed in the history of philosophy, in the chronology of debates, and in the bifurcations of the schools. ... What was important to Macedonio, however ... was not the circumstances and dates of philosophy, but

---

[24] Sarlo, *Jorge Luis Borges*, p 31
[25] Borges, *Poesía y poética*, no 15, p 61 (originally published in *Sur*, Nos 209-0 (March-April 1952)

philosophy itself.

Paul Celan, born into a Jewish family in Romania, in a poem published in the book *Nomansrose* in 1963, writes in German:

> There was earth inside them, and
> they dug.
>
> They dug and they dug, so their day
> went by for them, their night. And they did not praise God,
> who, so they heard, wanted all this
> ...
> They dug and heard nothing more;
> they did not grow wise, invented no song,
> thought up for themselves no language.[26]

The poem places pure materiality – the non-coded – on the inside: earth without inscription. 'Funes', if placed alongside that proposal, may be read not as an allegory of realism failing but as an exploration of an extreme, high-energy collision between language as inherited meanings – which shape memory and perception and thus make experience possible – and the force of the non-signifying.

Sarlo points out that Borges locates the scene of his writing as 'las orillas', that is at an in-between space where city and country, modernised present and rural past meet. And that from this space he generates intersections – mixtures – between Argentinian and European literature. What is the effect of the intersections? In 'History of the Warrior and the Captive', the place in between cultures – between the savage (Indian) and the civilised (Argentinian) – is 'dizzy':[27] the collision of mutually incompatible codings takes us to something that is not coded, to a zone that is a threshold of ecstasy (Borges uses that word). Not the savage outside, as in Kavafy's 'The Barbarians', nor the savage inside, as in Freud or Jung, but an indiscernible or multiple in-between.

In 'Funes the Memorious', the possibility of the ecstatic is continually pulled back into the narrator's archival, Romantic and monumental sensibility: his language enlists the rhetoric of official biographies, placing Funes inside the museum of national biography.[28]

---

[26] Paul Celan, *Poems of Paul Celan*, translated by Michael Hamburger (London, 1995 [1988]), p. 157.

[27] For Celine, the time, or space, between cultures is dangerous. See *Voyage au bout de la nuit* (1932). Borges's story has a double ambiguity: the savage is English – an English person captured by Indians. (I am grateful to Evelyn Fishburn for this observation).

[28] In 'Total recall: Texts and Corpses, the Museums of Argentinian Narrative', *Journal of Latin American Cultural Studies*, vol. 6, no. 1 (1997), pp. 21-32, Jens Andermann documents the creation of the Museum of La Plata as a state celebration of the Conquest of the Desert and shows how Macedonio Fernández and Borges invented memory spaces which are also reading machines

In a recent book, *The Politics of Time*, Peter Osborne, states the following:

> Modernity is our primary secular category of historical totalisation. But what justifies this totalisation of history, theoretically, if such an operation of necessity homogenises and represses, reduces or forgets, certain forms of difference?[29]

In 'Funes the Memorious', Borges writes:

> Pensar es olvidar diferencias, es generalisar, abstraer. En el aborrotado mundo de Funes no había sino detalles, casi inmediatos (*Ficciones*, p. 126).

> To think is to forget differences, generalise, make abstractions. In the teeming world of Funes, there were only details, almost immediate [in their presence].[30]

'Almost' is a key word in this passage and some of its force is taken away by the addition of 'in their presence' in the English translation. If the details in Funes's world were entirely immediate there would, in the strict sense, be no mediation (for example by the concept of 'presence'), that is, no intervention of any sign structures at all and thus, for example, no language. The 'almost' places Funes at a threshold, facing two ways, like the Yahoos in 'Doctor Brodie's Report' who can be read as simultaneously inside and outside language and culture. One can experiment with reading the two sentences just quoted in different directions. The second read from the first makes Funes's world a representation of incapacity due to lack of training – a lack of preparation which, read in the context of state imperatives in 1880s Argentina, looks like an incapacity for primary accumulation, a notorious defect of the semi-nomadic gaucho who, by the 1880s, had disappeared. But read from the second sentence, the first, lapidary sentence – Kant spoken by the monumental voice of La Patria – starts to sound hollow – like a need to sound monumental – and Funes's world can be read as the 'pre'-modern, like one of those general stores that has a bit of everything (*tienda de abarrotes*), like Pliny as opposed to Linnaeus, like pre-national literature as opposed to national literature, like time in Locke and Hume as opposed to time as told in the nineteenth century epic of progress which was emulated by the Argentine state bureaucracy. These are some of the places from which Borges's text produces readings of modernity.[31]

---

designed to counteract the effects of those museums of the nation established from the 1880s onwards.

[29] Peter Osborne, *The Politics of Time* (London: Verso, 1995) p. 29

[30] The translation, apart from the addition of square brackets, is from *Labyrinths*, p. 94.

[31] But not in a nostalgic way. Paul Feyerabend's anarchist episteme, for example, in *Against Method* (London. Verso, 1988), makes Borges into one of its precursors in the proposal of anti-bureaucratic knowledge· 'we need a dream-world in order to discover the features of the real world we think we inhabit'; 'no theory every agrees with all the facts in its domain' (pp 22-23, 29). Both Feyerabend and Thomas Kuhn (*The Structure of Scientific Revolutions*, Chicago, 1962) propose an anti-sacrificial relationship between knowledge and human beings

So it is a question of what is possible between the innumerable and the monumental in the reading machine. One reads the one from the other, in both directions, but in a condition of permanent non-completion. Holes are made in the compacted, monumental text of history, while the innumerable is made readable (writable), when read from a training in stable categories. Holes are then produced and make movement possible.[32] Instead of interpretation as selection that produces wholes, which is the model of reading proposed by Sarlo and practised by the narrator of the story, reading as a hole machine, producing endless interstices.

Conclusions

After this, is there a home base to come back to? What Borges leaves one with is not precisely a place from which to read. The endlessly in-between is not a place, whether place is a question of cultural geography or of concepts. As Proust wrote, 'We find that our wisdom begins where the author's ends; we would like him to give us answers, when all he can do is give us desires.'[33] If Borges displays, among other things, the effects of the state upon reading, that is where our wisdom has to begin. And the desires he leaves us with? They include, I suggest, a non-sacrificial relationship with language.

---

[32]   As molecular holes are used in microprocessors in order to move information The relationships between Borges's writing and the processes of electronic communication, which García Canclini points to in *Culturas híbridas. estrategias para entrar y salir de la modernidad* (Mexico City: Grijalbo, 1989), pp 103-8, are a subject that would be worth investigating.
[33]   'Nous sentons très bien que notre sagesse commence où celle de l'auteur finit, et nous voudrions qu'il nous donnât des réponses, quand tout ce qu'il peut faire est de nous donner des désirs.' Marcel Proust, *Sur la lecture* (Paris· Hubert Nyssen, 1994), p 32

CHAPTER 3

Borges: The Argentine Writer and the 'Western' Tradition[*]

Daniel Balderston

Borges is now officially part of the 'Western canon'. Harold Bloom, expert in such matters, includes him in the long list of canonical works in the appendix to his book of the same name,[1] and features Borges (along with Neruda and Pessoa) in a chapter with the curious title 'Borges, Neruda, and Pessoa: Hispano-Portuguese Whitmans'.[2] (Borges is one of only nine twentieth century writers discussed in the book, and out of a total of only twenty-six writers in all, so Bloom considers him quite canonical.) I don't know what Borges would have made of the company he keeps in Bloom's book – he barely knew of Pessoa and had famously mixed feelings about Neruda – much less of the 'Hispanic Whitmans' business.[3] Borges, of course, liked Whitman enough to devote several essays to him, but his writing is not very much like Whitman's, at least

[*] This chapter has appeared, in a different form and in Spanish, in *Cuadernos Americanos Nueva Epoca*, 64, Año XI, vol 4 (1997), pp. 167-78

[1] Harold Bloom, *The Western Canon. The Books and School of the Ages* (New York: Harcourt Brace, 1994).

[2] On this new version of the Holy Trinity, see Borges, 'Sobre el doblaje'. 'Las posibilidades del arte de combinar no son infinitas, pero suelen ser espantosas Los griegos engendraron la quimera, monstruo con cabeza de león, con cabeza de dragón, con cabeza de cabra, los teólogos del siglo II, la Trinidad, en la que inextricablemente se articulan el Padre, el Hijo y el Espíritu . .' (*Obras completas*, Buenos Aires Emecé, 1974, p 283).

[3] One of the many curiosities in Bloom's categorisation is this little gem of idiosyncratic, not to say mistaken, literary history

> Twentieth-century Hispanic American literature, possibly more vital than North American, has three founders. the Argentine fabulist Jorge Luis Borges (1899-1986); the Chilean poet Pablo Neruda (1904-1973), and the Cuban novelist Alejo Carpentier (1904-1980). Out of their matrix a host of major figures has emerged· novelists as varied as Julio Cortázor [sic], Gabriel García Márquez, Mario Vargas Llosa, and Carlos Fuentes; poets of international importance in César Vallejo, Octavio Paz, and Nicolás Guillén I center on Borges and Neruda, though time may demonstrate the supremacy of Carpentier over all other Latin American writers in this era But Carpentier was among the many indebted to Borges, and Neruda has the same founder's role for poetry that Borges occupies for both fictional and critical prose, so I examine them here both as literary fathers and representative writers (*The Western Canon*, p. 430)

At the very start of Bloom's chapter on 'Hispanic Whitmans' we encounter such bizarre and untrue notions as Vallejo's being born of Neruda, though there is a certain difficulty with chronology there.

Two other interesting examples of Bloom's ignorance of Latin American literature: he lists Sor Juana as a Spanish author (p. 503), not acknowledging that she lived in Mexico throughout her life (even if she did publish in Spain, like most of her Spanish American contemporaries), and argues vis-à-vis the historical novel. 'History writing and narrative fiction have come apart, and our sensibilities seem no longer able to accommodate them one to the other' (pp 20-1), a statement that rings completely false for the Latin Americ novel. In his list of nineteenth-century canonical works (pp 509-15) there are no Latin Americans whatsoever, not even Sarmiento or Machado de Assis not after about 1925.[4]

The real issue, here, is not whether Borges should be included in a 'Western canon' however limited or however large,[5] but what Borges does to the idea of canons. I will look first at his reflections on canonicity in 'Sobre los clásicos' (1965) [On the Classics] [6], then consider a particular example of his handling of a canonical text, Aristotle's *Poetics* (listed of course in Bloom's master list), in 'La busca de Averroes'[Averroes's Search]. Then I would like to return to 'El escritor argentino y la tradición', as suggested by my title, and ask what tradition is at stake here.

In 'Sobre los clásicos' Borges argues against an atemporal notion of the classic and the canon:

Clásico es aquel libro que una nación o un grupo de naciones o el largo tiempo han decidido leer como si en sus páginas todo fuera deliberado, fatal, profundo como el cosmos y capaz de interpretaciones sin término.[7] Previsiblemente, esas decisiones varían. Para los alemanes y austríacos el Fausto es una obra genial; para otros, una de las más famosas formas del tedio, como el segundo Paraíso de Milton o la obra de Rabelais (*Obras completas*, p. 773).

[A book becomes a classic when a nation or a group of nations or the passage of time has resolved to read it as if every word in it were deliberate, fated, profound as the cosmos and capable of endless interpretations. Predictably, these decisions vary. For the Germans and the Austrians, *Faust* is a work of genius: for others it is one of the most famous forms of tedium, like Milton's *Paradise Regained* or the writings of Rabelais.]

He adds: 'Una preferencia bien puede ser una superstición' [A preference may well be a form of superstition] (*Obras completas*, p. 773). The word 'superstición' will remind his faithful reader of the much earlier essay 'La supersticiosa ética del lector' [The Superstitious Habits of Readers] in *Discusión*, where he proposes that a lot of what passes for imaginative reading is actually stifled by obedience to custom and convention; certainly in this essay on

---

[4]   Bloom does know that Borges's earliest poetry aspired to be like Whitman's, but he bizarrely argues that Borges changed direction as a writer because Neruda 'powerfully usurped' the Whitman mantle (p. 430)

[5]   I am grateful to Irene Mathews for questioning the usefulness of Bloom's book, which of course I do not mean to validate as I quote from it. I consider Bloom's book important as a phenomenon in the 'culture wars' of recent years, absurd in its claims but interesting for what it reveals about the culture where it was produced.

[6]   The essay was added to late editions of *Otras inquisiciones*, a book originally published in 1952. The edition referred to is 1964 (Austin: University of Texas Press).

[7]   Cf Bloom: 'One ancient test for the canonical remains fiercely valid unless it demands rereading, the work does not qualify. The inevitable analogue is the erotic one. If you are Don Giovanni and Leporello keeps the list, one brief encounter will suffice' (p. 29).

the classics the words 'superstición' and 'tedio' are allied at the pole of the conventional.

Later in 'Sobre los clásicos', he expands on this idea:

> Las emociones que la literatura suscita son quizá eternas, pero los medios deben constantemente variar, siquiera de un modo levísimo, para no perder su virtud. Se gastan a medida que los reconoce el lector. De ahí el peligro de afirmar que existen obras clásicas y que lo serán para siempre (*Obras completas*, p. 773).

> [The emotions that literature evokes are perhaps eternal, but the means must vary constantly, be it never so slightly, so as not to lose their effect. They become worn by familiarity with each reading. This is why it is dangerous to state that there are classical works and that they will remain so forever.]

The essay concludes: 'Clásico no es un libro ... que necesariamente posee tales o cuales méritos; es un libro que las generaciones de los hombres, urgidas por diversas razones, leen con previo fervor y con una misteriosa lealtad' [A book is not classic because it possesses certain merits; it is a book that generations, urged on by diverse reasons, read with anticipated fervour and a mysterious loyalty] (p. 773); here, one should underline the word 'diversas', a word famously used in the last sentence of 'La esfera de Pascal' ['Pascal's Sphere'].

And à propos of Pascal's circle whose centre is nowhere and whose circumference is infinite, it is worth noting that in the stark centre of the campus of the University of São Paulo in Brazil, next to the clock, there is a marker that reads: 'NO UNIVERSO DA CULTURA O CENTRO ESTA EM TODA PARTE' [In the Universe of Culture the Centre is Everywhere]. This phrase, obviously not included by Borges in his census of variations on Pascal, is just as obviously the product of someone who read the Borges essay and appropriated it for a statement on Latin American culture. The centre is everywhere: Borges would have been pleased by this particular displacement of the canon, very much in keeping with his statements on the ways traditions are forged in such essays as 'Kafka y sus precursores' ['Kafka and his Precursors'] and 'Nota sobre (hacia) Bernard Shaw' ['For Bernard Shaw'], to say nothing of the more obvious 'Sobre los clásicos' and 'El escritor argentino y la tradición' ['The Argentine Writer and Tradition'].

The notion, so passionately argued in 'Sobre los clásicos', that it is not only rereading but constant rereading with a difference, wreaks havoc with conventional ideas of the canon, including Bloom's. He is all for rereading, but rereading should merely deepen one's understanding that Shakespeare 'anchors' the canon because his characters change, that Dante is the other 'anchor' because his characters are fixed once and for all, and so forth. Of Borges, for instance, he writes:

> A dread of what Freud called the family romance and of what might be
> termed the family romance of literature confines Borges to repetition,
> and to overidealization of the writer-reader relationship. That may be
> precisely what made him the ideal father for modern Hispanic-
> American literature – his infinite suggestiveness and his detachment
> from cultural tangles. Yet he may be condemned to a lesser eminence,
> still canonical but no longer central, in modern literature. A comparison
> of his stories and parables to Kafka's, read side by side, is not at all
> flattering to him but seems inevitable, partly because Borges so
> frequently invokes Kafka, both overtly and implicitly. Beckett, with
> whom Borges shared an international prize in 1961, at his best sustains
> intense rereading as Borges does not. Borges' cunning is adroit but does
> not sustain a Schopenhauerian vision as powerfully as Beckett is able to
> do (*The Western Canon*, p. 438).[8]

There are several things wrong here. First, Bloom is utterly blind to the
particular use that Borges makes of repetition, for repetition in Borges is – as he
shows most clearly in 'Pierre Menard' – always the site of difference, of
divergence. Second, the fact that Borges seems more inclined to 'embrace' than
to murder his precursors makes him anathema to Bloom because he does not fit
the pattern laid out so many years ago in *The Anxiety of Influence*,[9] but does not
make him a lesser writer; in fact, his manner of weaving text and allusion has
proved fruitful for many other writers and artists, and fascinating to untold
numbers of readers and critics. And third, the matter of rereading itself: far be it
from me to say how anyone else should reread, but I have never found any text
so different each time I approach it, yet again an 'undiscovered country', as
Borges's.

Borges is, as Bloom recognises, central to 'the Western canon' because of his
inclusive relation to it, though Bloom's tired Oedipal model questions whether
this is healthy: 'Borges . . . overtly absorbs and then reflects the entire canonical
tradition. Whether this open embrace of his precursors finally curtailed Borges'
achievement is a difficult question' (*The Western Canon*, p. 432). Bloom sees
Borges as insufficiently agonistic, and agon, as we know, is at the centre of
Bloom's vision of the world. Borges's world, like Pascal's sphere or the motto at
the University of São Paulo, has a moveable centre that can be anywhere.

Nowhere is this sensation of difference, of displacement, sharper than in 'La
busca de Averroes', the 1947 story in *El aleph*.[10] Aristotle's *Poetics* is the

---

[8]   Bloom continues: 'Nevertheless, Borges' position in the Western Canon, if it prevails, will be
as secure as Kafka's and Beckett's. Of all Latin American authors in this century, he is the most
universal' (p. 439). What sort of 'universality' does Bloom claim for Borges?

[9]   Harold Bloom, *The Anxiety of Influence: A Theory of Poetics* (Oxford and London: Oxford
University Press, 1975).

[10]   What follows is an abridged version of my article 'Borges, Averroes, Aristotle: The Poetics of

founding text of 'Western' literary criticism and theory (even if Bloom prefers as point of origin Aristophanes's reflections on Euripides (*The Western Canon*, p. 171), so it is interesting to see what Borges does with canons in this story. His Averroes, hard at work on his commentary (presumably the surviving middle commentary) on the *Poetics*, is disturbed by a 'philological' doubt related to his commentary on the *Poetics* at the moment he is penning the eleventh chapter of his *Tahafut Al-Tahafut* (*Incoherence of the Incoherence*), his attack on al-Ghazali's *Tahafut Al-Filasifa* (*Incoherence of the Philosophers*), in its turn an attack on philosophy as an illegitimate branch of theology. This 'philological' doubt, that serves to interrupt Averroes's philosophy for an afternoon and an evening, has to do with two unknown words, 'tragedy' and 'comedy'. Now, any reader of Aristotle's *Poetics* will concur that an inability to decipher these words will gravely impede an understanding of Aristotle's text, and Averroes shares that preoccupation: 'Esas dos palabras arcanas pululaban en el texto de la Poética; imposible eludirlas' (*Obras completas*, p. 583) [These two arcane words pullulated throughout the text of the *Poetics*; it was impossible to elude them (*Labyrinths*, p. 181)].[11]

Much of the Borges story is a discussion with Abulcásim al-Asharí (the name is based on that of one of Averroes's biographers) about whether it is better to show or to tell. Al-Asharí tells of his experience of having attended a theatre in China – 'Imaginemos que alguien muestra una historia en vez de referirla' (p. 585) [Let us imagine that someone performs a story instead of telling it. (*Labyrinths*, p. 184)] – and because he does not tell of the experience in a way that is clearly understandable (even to Averroes, who is hungry for information about precisely this art, though he may not know it), the consensus among his listeners is that it is unnecessary to use numerous people to tell a story when one would suffice. The issue arises in the *Poetics*, in the passage cited by Borges in 'El pudor de la historia' ['A Modesty of History'], when Aristotle recalls that Aeschylus increased the number of actors from one to two;[12] Borges comments on this passage at some length, finally noting:

> nunca sabremos si [Esquilo] presintió, siquiera de un modo imperfecto, lo significativo de aquel pasaje del uno al dos, de la unidad a la pluralidad y así a lo infinito. Con el segundo actor entraron el diálogo y las indefinidas posibilidades de la reacción de unos carácteres sobre otros (*Obras completas*, pp. 754-5).

> [we shall never know if (Aeschylus) had a prefiguring, even an imperfect one, of the importance of that passage from one to two, from unity to plurality and thus to infinity. With the second actor came the dialogue and the indefinite possiblities of the reaction of some

---

Poetics', which appeared in *Hispania* (1996)
[11]   Borges, *Labyrinths* (Harmondsworth: Penguin Books, 1970).
[12]   Aristotle, *Poetics*, trans. with notes and intro by Richard Janko (Indianapolis: Hackett Publishing Company, 1987), p. 6

characters on others (*Other Inquisitions*, p. 168)].[13]

The same issue – showing versus telling – now wholly transposed into the art of narrative, preoccupied Henry James and his followers, notably Percy Lubbock. In Borges's story, Farach, the scholar of the *Koran*, says of the Chinese theatre that has been described by his guest Albucásim: 'En tal caso ... no se requerían *veinte* personas. Un solo hablista puede referir cualquier cosa, por compleja que sea' (*Obras completas*, p. 586) [In that case ... twenty persons are unnecessary. One single speaker can tell anything, no matter how complicated it might be (*Labyrinths*, p. 185)].

But the central point of the story is, as the narrator states at the end, 'el proceso de una derrota, ... el caso de un hombre que se propone un fin que no está vedado a los otros, pero sí a él' (*Obras completas*, pp. 587-8) [the process of defeat ... the case of a man who sets himself a goal which is not forbidden to others, but is to him (*Labyrinths*, p. 187)]. For the narrator, and presumably for the reader, a reading of Aristotle's *Poetics* by someone without knowledge and experience of the theatre is unthinkable, but such is the case of Averroes in twelfth-century Al-Andalus. Ironically, of course, the narrator calls attention to boys in the street pretending to be muezzin and congregation (playing, that is, at the theatre), and the conversation at Farach's house, as we have seen, turns on Abulcásim's account of a visit to a theatre in China. A reading of the *Poetics* by someone who thinks that tragedy is panegyric or eulogy and comedy is satire seems ludicrous, as Renan remarks in his *Averroès et l'averroïsme* (in the same passage from which Borges took the epigraph to the story): 'Cette paraphrase accuse ... l'ignorance la plus complète de la littérature grecque'.[14]

Let me now confess to having read Averroes's *Middle Commentary on Aristotle's Poetics*, translated into English in 1986 by Charles E. Butterworth.[15] This work, as Butterworth notes, is almost unknown in the Arabic-speaking world, having only been published in the last 125 years and in scholarly editions that have apparently circulated little; the two Arabic manuscripts are preserved in libraries in Florence and Leiden. Renan knew the work through translations of translations of the original, remarking at one point that the works of Averroes that were available to him were Latin translations of Hebrew translations of a commentary made upon Arabic translations of Syriac translations of Greek originals (*Averroès*, p. 52); Averroes's inability to read Aristotle directly is more than compensated by his readers' inability (from Thomas Aquinas to Borges) to read him directly. If it were not for Butterworth's notes, Averroes's quotations from and reflections on Arabic poetry and poetics would be nearly incomprehensible for the Western non-Arabist reader (as they were for one of his medieval translators, Hermann Alemann)[16], just as Averroes could not make

---

[13]   Borges, *Other Inquisitions*, trans. Ruth L.C. Simms (Austin and London: University of Texas Press, 1964).

[14]   Ernest Renan, *Averroès et l'averroïsme* (Paris: Calmann-Lévy, n. d.), p 48.

[15]   Princeton: Princeton University Press, 1986

[16]   See Butterworth's introduction to his translation of the *Middle Commentary* (p. xii) and Renan,

much sense of Aristotle's references to Greek poetry. But this is not entirely the point. Averroes acknowledges at the outset that Aristotle comments on aspects of Greek poetry that do not have ready analogies in Arabic poetry, or in the poetry of 'most or all nations', to use his frequent phrase; he sets as his task the adaptation of Aristotle's argument to Arabic poetry. Thus, he argues through his commentary that Aristotle did not set out the rules for all poetry and that he will not do so either; the *Poetics* and the *Middle Commentary* are particular rather than general in scope.

In one of his essays on Dante, Borges writes: 'La precisión que acabo de indicar no es un artificio retórico; es afirmación de la probidad, de la plentitud, con que cada incidente del poema ha sido imaginado' [The precision that I have just pointed out is not a rhetorical device; it is an affirmation of the probity, the plentitude, with which each incident in the poem has been imagined].[17] In the case of Borges's 'Averroes', what is at stake in arguing for 'precision' is not the minimal references to the local colour of Moslem Spain – the fountain, the harem and so forth – but the intellectual rigour with which Averroes's mental world has been recreated: the right chapter of the *Tahafut* is mentioned, the names of the Arabic translators of Aristotle are correctly cited, the Hellenistic commentator on Aristotle (Alexander of Aphrodisias) is consulted at the right moment. John Sturrock gets it profoundly wrong when he calls Borges's erudition into question here, doubting the existence of Alexander of Aphrodisias and stating of the Ghazali *Tahafut* and of Averroes's reply: 'Whether these are real works of early Arabic thought, or whether Borges has made them up, I do not know. Their existence is, so to speak, immaterial'.[18] On the contrary: Borges may not have known how to read Arabic or Hebrew but he made excellent use of the Latin and modern material (not, as Sturrock would have it, 'immaterial') available to him.

'Pierre Menard', like 'La fruición literaria' ['Literary Pleasures'] before it, complicates the matter of literary interpretation by insisting that the meaning of a text depends not only on the conditions of its production (who wrote it, when, and under what circumstances) but also of its reception. In this story the same idea is broached in the discussion of whether a metaphor in a classic Arabic poem (destiny seen as a blind camel) has become a mere cliché; Averroes argues to the contrary that an image penned in the Arabian desert acquires new layers of meaning centuries later in Al-Andalus: 'Dos términos tenía la figura y hoy tiene cuatro' (*Obras completas*, p. 587) [the figure had two terms then and now it has four (*Labyrinths*, p. 186)]. The two new terms added to the figure (which initially consisted of 'camel' and 'destiny') are 'Zuhair', the Arabic poet who composed the image,[19] and 'nuestros pesares', the sufferings and sorrows of

---

Averroès (pp 211-2).

[17] Borges, *Nueve ensayos dantescos* (Madrid. Espasa-Calpe, 1982), p. 88.

[18] John Sturrock, 'Between Commentary and Comedy. The Satirical Side of Borges', in Claude Rawson (ed.), *English Satire and the Satiric Tradition* (Oxford· Basil Blackwell, 1984), pp. 279 and 280.

[19] On Zuhair, see Butterworth's note on a different quotation from this poet (*Middle Commentary*

Zuhair's Spanish readers, so distant from the Arabian desert. By the same token, Aristotle's text is enriched on being read by Averroes, and Averroes's on being read by Borges, although the 'difference' between one and another may be as invisible as that between Menard's and Cervantes's versions of 'la verdad, cuya madre es la historia' (*Obras completas*, p. 449) [truth, whose mother is history (*Labyrinths*, p. 69)].

'La busca de Averroes', then, is the story of the founding text of literary theory, as misunderstood – or better still, as reimagined – in a different cultural context. The story is cast as a tragedy in Aristotle's terms: the philosopher's quest is undone by his ignorance, and by his masking of his ignorance with a sense of superiority. For undertaking a translation of the *Poetics* without a sense of what theatre is (much less the distinction between tragedy and comedy) is surely an act of hubris. Averroes's failure ('quise narrar el proceso de una derrota' (*Obras comletas*, p. 587) [I tried to narrate the process of a defeat (*Labyrinths*, p. 187)]) is mirrored in the narrator's failure, Averroes's disappearance before the mirror signalling the failure of the narrator's imagination.

Renan, reading Latin translations of Hebrew translations of an Arabic commentary on Syriac translations of a Greek original: what is interesting in this chain is not only the distance that separates Renan from Averroes, and Averroes from Aristotle, but also the sustained attention to the object at the other end of the chain. Like the rows of translators in the Inca Garcilaso's account of the de Soto expedition to Florida, this attention implies – hope against hope – the possibility of communication. Aristotle may be ultimately as distant from us as Averroes, yet Borges, with his characteristic generosity, invites us to make the crossing.

And yet in this distance or loss there is also gain: Averroes's discussion of metaphor is richer than Aristotle's (though the non-Arabist reader may have to rely on Butterworth's notes to make full sense of it), and Borges opens new discursive spaces by blurring genealogies and points of origin. When Averroes recalls his Moroccan exile in the story, he says:

Así, atormentado hace años en Marrakesh por memorias de Córdoba, me complacía en repetir el apóstrofe que Abdurrahmán dirigió en los jardines de Ruzafa a una palma africana:

> Tú también eres, ¡oh palma!
> En este suelo extranjera. . .

Singular beneficio de la poesía; palabras redactadas por un rey que anhelaba el Oriente me sirvieron a mí, desterrado en Africa, para mi nostalgia de España (*Obras completas*, p. 587).

---

p. 61).

[Thus when I was tormented years ago in Marrakesh by memories of Cordova, I took the pleasure in repeating the apostrophe Abdurrahman addressed in the gardens of Ruzafa to an African palm:

> You too, oh palm! are
> Foreign to this soil ...

The singular benefit of poetry: words composed by a king who longed for the Orient served me, exiled in Africa, to express my nostalgia for Spain (*Labyrinths*, p. 186)].

This parable within the larger story serves to sharpen the focus on the problem of origin and belonging. Does Averroes's thought 'descend' from Aristotle's? Does ours? The answer in both cases is emphatically no: there is no 'natural' line of descent possible here, only the constant reinvention of tradition, what Borges elsewhere calls the making of precursors. Averroes makes Aristotle strange because he does not have the experience of the theatre, but Aristotle is quite as strange for those of us who do, as a look at the scholarly controversies around the *Poetics* will show. And it is actually in this 'making strange' that Borges is closest to Bloom (or perhaps that Bloom is closest to Borges, since *The Anxiety of Influence* and its many sequels, including this one, arguably derive from 'Kafka y sus precursores', since Bloom argues near the end of *The Western Canon* (just before the notorious list), that 'ambivalences define centrality in a canonical context' (p. 491). Shortly after this, he adds:

> a canon is an *achieved* anxiety, just as any strong literary work is its author's achieved anxiety. The literary canon does not baptize us into culture; it does not make us free of cultural anxiety. Rather, it confirms our cultural anxieties, yet helps to give them form and coherence (*The Western Canon*, p. 492).

One of the central anxieties produced by the idea of canons is that experienced by the reader, even the professional or academic reader, caused by that library of unread or half-remembered books. This problem is perhaps most acute in the New World (and in the post-colonial world in general), because of conflicts over what our cultural heritage is, the problem that Borges puzzled over in 'El escritor argentino y la tradición'. Bloom's response, like E. D. Hirsch's in *The Culture of Literacy* (and, for that matter, like Ezra Pound's in *The ABC of Reading)*,[20] is to make a long list, which surely will only make some of his readers more anxious (and others furious). Borges displaces the question from convention or tradition to individual taste: near the end of 'Sobre los clásicos' he writes: 'Libros como el de Job, la Divina Comedia, Macbeth (y, para mí, algunas de las sagas del Norte) prometen una larga inmortalidad, pero nada sabemos del porvenir, salvo que diferirá del presente' (*Obras completas*, p. 773) [Books such as Job, the *Divine Comedy*, *Macbeth* (and for me Norse Sagas)

---

[20]   C D. Hirsh, *Cultural Literacy· What Every American Needs to Know* (Boston· Houghton Mifflin, 1987), Ezra Pound, *The ABC of Reading* (London: Faber, 1991).

promise a long immortality, but we know nothing of the future other than that it will differ from the present] or later still, and in an even more personal tone: 'Yo, que me he resignado a poner en duda la indefinida perduración de Voltaire o de Shakespeare, creo (esta tarde de uno de los últimos días de 1965) en la de Schopenhauer y en la de Berkeley' (*Obras completas,* p. 773) [I, who have resigned myself to question the everlasting survival of Voltaire or Shakespeare, yet believe (on this afternoon of one of the last days of 1965) in the survival of Schopenhauer and Berkeley]. The particularity of these assertions, the fact that they are spoken in the first person singular and, in the later case, even dated, serves to displace the question of universality or even commonality onto one of personal taste and loyalty. I think there can be no doubt that Borges would have been amused by Bloom's earnest lists and furious tone, and would have begged off with a humourous aside at being canonised in this best-selling book, brushing off Bloom in the same tone he used in 'Las alarmas del doctor Américo Castro' ['Dr Americo Castro is Alarmed']: 'En la página 122, el doctor Castro ha enumerado algunos escritores [argentinos] cuyo estilo es correcto; a pesar de la inclusión de mi nombre en ese catálogo, no me creo del todo incapacitado para hablar de estilística' (*Obras completas,* p. 657) [On page 122 Dr Castro has enumerated several writers whose style is correct. In spite of the inclusion of my name on that list, I do not consider myself entirely unqualified to speak of stylistics (*Other Inquisitions,* p. 30)].

In 'El escritor argentino y la tradición', Borges writes that for such writers as Shaw, Berkeley and Swift 'les bastó el hecho de sentirse irlandeses, distintos, para innovar en la cultura inglesa' (*Obras completas,* p. 273) [it was sufficient for them to feel Irish, to feel different, in order to be innovators in English culture. (*Labyrinths,* p. 218)], and makes the same argument for the primacy of Jewish writers in Europe in general. He then continues, famously: 'Creo que los argentinos, los sudamericanos, estamos en una situación análoga; podemos manejar todos los temas europeos, manejarlos sin supersticiones, con una irreverencia que puede tener, y ya tiene, consecuencias afortunadas' (*Obras completas,* p. 273) [I believe that we Argentines, we South Americans in general, are in an anaologous situation: we can handle all European themes, handle them without superstition, with an irreverence which can have, and already does have, fortunate consequences (*Labyrinths,* p. 218)].

And in that essay, which is of course a response to Peronist questioning of whether Borges was sufficiently Argentine as a writer,[21] Borges sets out a programme of sorts, but it is a programme that upsets fixed ideas of canon and tradition:

---

[21] See for instance Fermín Chávez's *Civilización y barbarie en la cultura argentina* (1956; 2nd. edn. Buenos Aires· Ediciones Theoría, 1965), in which Chávez attacks Borges for his 'denigración de lo original en provecho de lo espurio' [denigrating the original in favour of the spurious] (p. 41), for his 'buena literatura borgiana pero no muy argentina' [illegitimate good borgesian but not very Argentine literature] (p 37). I am grateful to Julio Ramos for having pointed out that 'El escritor argentino y la tradición', presented in 1951, is clearly a response to the polemics among Argentine intellectuals that were provoked by the cultural nationalism of the Perón government.

no debemos temer y ... debemos pensar que nuestro patrimonio es el universo; ensayar todos los temas, y no podemos concretarnos a lo argentino para ser argentinos: porque o ser argentino es una fatalidad y en ese caso lo seremos de cualquier modo, o ser argentino es una mera afectación, una máscara. Creo que si nos abandonamos a ese sueño voluntario que se llama la creación artística, seremos argentinos y seremos, también, buenos o tolerables escritores (*Obras completas*, p. 274).

[we should not be alarmed and .... we should feel that our patrimony is the universe; we should essay all themes, and we cannot limit ourselves to purely Argentine subjects in order to be Argentine; for either being Argentine is an inescapable act of fate – and in that case we shall be so in all events – or being Argentine is a mere affectation, a mask. I believe that if we surrender ourselves to that voluntary dream which is artistic creation, we shall be Argentine and we shall be good or tolerable writers (*Labyrinths*, p. 219)].

This argument for freedom from constraint, whether nationalist or pedagogical, is Borges's response to his local version of what Bloom calls 'the School of Resentment', which probably includes most of readers of this volume, and which curiously marks him most of all, since he wears his agon on his sleeve.

In 'La fruición literaria', the 1928 essay on reading in *El idioma de los argentinos*,[22] Borges anticipates in a curious way the argument of his 1947 story 'El inmortal' ['The Immortal'] (originally entitled, as here, 'Los inmortales' ['The Immortals']). After noting that 'El tiempo – amigo de Cervantes –ha sabido corregirle las pruebas' (p. 92) [Time – the friend of Cervantes – has often corrected his drafts], he adds:

En general, el destino de los inmortales es otro. Los pormenores de su sentir o de su pensar suelen desvanecerse o yacen invisibles en su labor, irrecuperables e insospechados. En cambio, su individualidad (esa simplificadísima idea platónica que en ningún rato de su vida fueron con pureza) se aferra como una raíz a las almas. Se vuelven pobres y perfectos como un guarismo. Se hacen abstracciones. Son apenas un manojito de sombra, pero lo son con eternidad (p. 92).

[In general, the destiny of immortals is different. The details of their feelings or of their thoughts tend to fade or to lie unnoticed in their work, irretrievable and unsuspected. Instead, their individuality (that extremely simplified Platonic idea that at no stage in their lives did they exist in a pure form) clings like a root to their souls. They become poor

---

[22] Borges, 'La fruición literaria' in his volume *El idioma de los argentinos* (Barcelona: Gleizer, 1928), pp 87-93

and perfect, like a cipher. They become abstractions. They are mere shadows, but they are so eternally].

Bloom writes of 'El inmortal':

> We surmise, at the story's end, that the singularly vague features are those of the Immortal, the poet Homer himself, who has merged with the Roman tribune and finally (by implication) with Borges himself, even as the story, 'The Immortal', merges Borges with his originals: De Quincey, Poe, Kafka, Shaw, Chesterton, Conrad, and several more (*The Western Canon*, pp. 439-40).

A page later he adds: 'Partly Borges is satirizing *Back to Methuselah*, but he is also savaging his own literary idealism. Without rivalry and polemic between the Immortals there is, paradoxically, no life, and literature dies'. Thanks to polemical rereadings, including Bloom's, there can be no doubt now, a decade after Borges's death in Geneva, that his work is alive.

CHAPTER 4

Hidden Pleasures in Borges's Allusions[*]

Evelyn Fishburn

Ya no nos quedan más que citas. La lengua es un sistema de citas.

J.L.Borges, *'Utopía de un hombre que está cansado'*

Ce qu'il importe, ce n'est pas de dire, d'est de redire, et, dans cette redite, de dire chaque fois encore une première fois.

Maurice Blanchot, *L'Entretien infini*

Allusions were (indirectly) linked to pleasure by Freud when, in *Beyond the Pleasure Principle*[1] he placed the origin of the sign and of meaning in the repetition element in the *fort-da* game. Every repetition is a form of allusion to a previous experience converting it into a symbol. Each time the experience is recalled there is pleasure, not only in having mastered the sign, being in command of it, as it were, but also of re-using the already known for an anticipated further pleasure. Antoine Compagnon, in his exhaustive and excellent study of 'la citation'[2] compares the pleasure or the comfort of quotations to what Winnicott has termed *transitional objects* or *not-me possessions*. Like the corner of an old blanket , or the favourite Teddy the child drags along for security, so do we use an allusion and shelter in its security as we venture forth to say something of our own. Many of Borges's stories commence with this sheltering behind a profusion of allusions but it need hardly be pointed out that if Borges invokes a great number of cultural references it is not only as the result of 'an incurable shyness' (of which he has spoken on several occasions) but also, which is quite the opposite, the manifestation of a spirit of daring and subversiveness against the supposed authority of the original source. It is what Harold Bloom, in his important work on the anxiety of influence has termed 'creative misreading'.[3] Quotations and allusions in Borges's work act on a double level: as an apparent site of refuge (mainly in traditional Western culture) but a refuge that becomes transformed when a

[*]   This chapter has appeared, in a different form and in Spanish, in *Cuadernos Americanos Nueva Epoca*, 64, Año XI, vol 4 (1997), pp 195-203
[1]   Sigmund Freud, *Beyond the Pleasure Principle* (London and Vienna· International Psychoanalytical Press, 1922).
[2]   Antoine Compagnon, *La Seconde main, ou, le travail de la citation* (Paris: Seuil, 1979).
[3]   Harold Bloom, *The Anxiety of Influence A Theory of Poetry* (New York: Oxford University Press, 1973)

contrary sense to that of the original is given to the allusion. Thus, what began as justification is destabilised and the allusion opens up to a new dialogue between the two contexts, the original and the new. In this sense, Borges seems to push to its limits Gracián's spirited suggestion that one may quote without necessarily remaining faithful. When this occurs, in the words of González Echevarría, 'it means the disappearance of anteriority and authority, of a transcendental signified'[4] and we have instead an innovative interplay between what has been said and what is being said.

The object of this study is not to establish the presence of any particular influences[5] or to find an overarching theory which would seek to read uniformity or a system into Borges's use of allusion. Instead, my intention is to look at the possibilities of new readings when the veiled implications of an allusion are made explicit, or a particular allusion is either examined in its own cultural context or traced to its original source. Allusions operate in a variety of ways and the categories given below are as arbitrary as those of 'a certain Chinese encyclopedia' and should be treated with the same sense of amusement.[6] They range from the teasing veiled allusion meant as a private joke, to be shared with some readers, but bearing no particular significance upon the general reading of a story;[7] to those that encapsulate its main gist, adding at times an ironic twist to it; to those hidden in the pages of a hinted source, offering unexpected new angles from which a story might be re-read. Needless to say, these categories overlap and intertwine at every stage. Erudition, appositeness and humour are their hallmark.

Veiled allusions, teasing the reader: there are many of these in Borges's stories, the most famous being to Franz Kafka spelt as Qaphqa in 'La lotería en Babilonia' ['The Babylon Lottery']. The mock-Aramaic transliteration gives the Czech name a Middle Eastern ring.

In 'El acercamiento a Almotásim' [The Approach to Al-Mu'tasim'] we learn of some detective novels by the seemingly unknown author John H Watson. This is an oblique reference to Dr. Watson, of 'elementary, my dear Watson'; fame, resting upon the fact that the first Sherlock Holmes story was presented as

---

[4]   Roberto González Echevarría, 'Borges and Derrida', in Harold Bloom (ed.), *Jorge Luis Borges* (New York, New Haven and Philadelphia: Chelsea House Publishers, 1968), p. 233.

[5]   This important work has been undertaken by a number of critics, amongst whom R. Christ, *The Narrow Act Borges' Art of Allusion* (New York Lumen Books, revised 1995, 1st published 1968); Gene Bell Villada, *Borges and his Fiction* (Chapel Hill· North Carolina Univ Press, 1981); Daniel Balderston, *El precursor velado R L Stevenson en la obra de Borges* (Buenos Aires: Sudamericana, 1985) and *Out of Context Historical Reference and the Representation of Reality in Borges* (Durham and London Duke University Press, 1993); S Molloy, *Signs of Borges* (Durham and London Duke University Press, 1994). Many of the ideas discussed in this article are based on research done in connection with E Fishburn and P Hughes, *A Dictionary of Borges* (London: Duckworth, 1990)

[6]   Borges, *Other Inquisitions* (Austin and London University of Texas Press, 1964), p. 103 For 'the shattering laughter' produced by this passage and its philosophical consequences, read the preface to Michel Foucault, *Les Mots et les choses* (Paris: Gallimard, 1966)

[7]   See Christ, *Narrow Act*, p 280

'a *reprint* from the reminiscences of John H. Watson' who has remained as the chronicler of the rest. So, perversely, because of the word 'reprint', Watson is recalled correctly as an author and most readers are misled. Relating to Freud's contention that for humour to operate there must be a shared language, these are two examples of many jokes giving pleasure to the reader who has understood, and establishing an added intimacy between this reader and the author. The story's meaning is hardly affected by this information.

Local criollo references

One of the reasons why *El informe de Brodie* [*Dr. Brodie's Report*] has not had the critical acclaim that it merits is that many of its subtleties have been overlooked either by lack of familiarity with the local context or by inattention to its detail. For example, at the end of 'La historia de Rosendo' ['Rosendo's Tale'] the *compadrito* who refused to be drawn into a fight goes away, eventually coming back to settle in San Telmo, que 'ha sido siempre un barrio de orden' (p. 48) [San Telmo always was a respectable neighbourhood (*Br.*, p. 51)].[8] The standard interpretation is that 'Rosendo' is a more mature version of 'El hombre de la esquina rosada' ['Streetcorner Man'] where the fight famously does take place, because in this story the cycle of street-fighting has been broken in favour of peacefulness. Yet San Telmo, though today a tourist attraction because of its old colonial architecture, is according to legend a place of rough and swaggering machismo, as boasted in the popular song: *Soy del barrio de San Telmo/ donde* llueve *y no gotea/ a mí no me asustan bultos / ni grupos que se menean* (emphasis added) [I am from San Telmo/ where it *rains* and does not drizzle/ I am not scared by shifting shapes or groups of people]. Read with this information in mind, the ending acquires an ironic twist since the *barrio*'s alleged peacefulness becomes severely questioned.

Allusions in epigraphs

Epigraphs, traditionally, serve to summarise or encapsulate the main theme of the work they head, but seldom so in Borges, where they are more likely to stand in humorous or ironic counterpoise to the core story. The epigraph of 'Deutsches Requiem', taken from The Book of Job and not easily explicable in this context, is one such example. The words quoted are 'Though He slay me, yet will I trust in Him' but Borges gives as his source the complete verse (Job, 13:15) which concludes with the following declaration of faith: 'but I will maintain mine own ways before Him'. I should like to suggest that these omitted words provide the tacit link between Job and the German character Zur Linde, whose faith in

---

8   References to Borges's *Ficciones*, *El aleph* and *El informe de Brodie* are to the *Obras completas* (Buenos Aires: Emecé, 1956, 1957 and 1970 respectively). The translations cited are *Labyrinths* (Harmondsworth Penguin Books, 1970), *A Personal Anthology* and *Doctor Brodie's Report* (Harmondsworth. Penguin Books, 1972) and *The Aleph And Other Stories, 1933-1969* (London: Picador, 1973) Unacknowledged translations are my own

Nazism is not less absolute than Job's in God. The virulence of the trials to which Job is submitted are mirrored by the atrocities witnessed by Zur Linde and interpreted by him as necessary to what he considers a moral cause, the salvation of Germany. Job's 'Behold now, I have ordered my cause, I know I shall be justified' (Job, 13:18) can be seen, perversely repeated in Zur Linde's assertion 'a mí me regocija que nuestro don sea orbicular y perfecto' *(El aleph*, p. 89*)* [I rejoice in the fact that our destiny completes its circle and is perfect *(Labyrinths*, p. 179)]. The parallel, however should not be abused, but taken as an ironic reflection on self-delusion seen at the meeting point between religious fervour and fanaticism.

Borges felt deep admiration for Job, a book he considered 'essential'.[9] In a lecture delivered at the Argentine-Israeli Cultural Institute in Buenos Aires Borges expanded on the main interpretations of the story of Job, quoting Quevedo's reading according to which the biblical tale is a prefiguration of Christ and 'the still to come martyrs of future days', an insight that provides a thematic link with 'Deutsches Requiem' where the Jewish poet David Jerusalem is hounded to death.[10] Needless to say, the solace offered at the end of The Book of Job is not to be found in Borges's story.

Allusion in proper nouns

Borges's choice of some of his characters' names has often led to conjecture as to their origins and status. Very few appear to have been picked randomly and in many cases an invented name has, by association, fulfilled some particular role. There has been much speculation about the name Pierre Menard: baker, riddler, graphologist who corresponded with Freud are some of the suggestions given.[11] There is no knowing which if any of these is meant, but there are possibilities of establishing connections with historical Menards either on the basis of intentionality or coincidence. The surname has several entries in the *Grand Larousse encyclopédique* in which one or other precursoring feature can be

---

[9]   *Siete noches, Obras completas 1975-1985* (Buenos Aires: Emecé, 1989), p. 216; see too p. 272. For other instances when Borges expressed the importance he attached to the Book of Job, see Edna Aizenberg, *The Aleph Weavers Biblical, Kabbalistic, and Judaic Elements in Borges* (Potomac, Md.: Scripta Humanistica, 1984), pp 78-9

[10]   Borges discusses two further interpretations· one, prevalent in the nineteenth century, focuses on the story as a discussion on the problems of evil, making a connection between Job and Greek tragedy, and the other, Borges's own favoured interpretation, sees the Biblical story as an illustration of the inscrutability of God See J L Borges, *Conferencias* (Buenos Aires: Instituto de Intercambio Cultural Argentino-Israelí, 1967), pp 93-102. We are indebted to E. Aizenberg for making this text available in edited translation in her *Borges and His Successors The Borges Impact on Literature and the Arts* (Columbia and London: University of Missouri Press, 1990), pp. 263-75.

[11]   Emir Rodríguez Monegal, *Literary Biography* (New York. Dutton, 1978), p. 123, argues in favour of Louis on the basis that Borges may have read about him in De Gourmont's *Promenades littéraires* and *Promenades philosophiques* whereas Daniel Balderston, slightly tongue in cheek, claims a connection with a Dr. Pierre Menard, a graphologist whom Borges reputedly met while on a visit to Nîmes See Balderston, *Out of Context*, pp. 19-38.

imaginatively detected. For instance, there was a Léon who was relevantly involved in the history of Nîmes and a Louis whose version in French verse of Aeschylus's tragedy *Prométhée délivré* (1843), may be a genetic sign of predisposition for Pierre Menard's 'transposición en alejandrinos del *Cimetière marin*' de Paul Valéry *(Ficciones* , p. 47*)* [transposition into alexandrines of Paul Valéry's *Le Cimetière marin*]. Moreover, in 1896, Louis re-issued his own 'Les Rêveries d'un païen mystique', written some twenty years earlier, with the slightly changed title 'Poèmes et rêveries d'un païen mystique'. The Larousse adds the comment that 'par une fantaisie paradoxale il les a fait imprimer en nouvelle orthographe, ce qui les a empêché de trouver auprès du public lettré le grand succès qu'ils méritent'. Pierre Menard, of course, was obsessively preoccupied with re-issues, and if not of new spelling, at least of new punctuation. These details of coincidence are not meant to tie down Borges's character, so rich in literary associations, to any particular precursor of that name but rather to demonstrate the possibilities of a two-way 'traffic' in Borges's allusions. For, in the wake of 'Pierre Menard, autor del Quijote' [Pierre Menard, Author of the Quixote], the Larousse entries assume a different meaning, thereby illustrating the imaginative readings proposed in the 'obra invisible' of the symbolist poet from Nîmes.

An example where a name acts as a cryptic clue to a particular interpretation of a story can be found in the patronym of the narrator of the events described in 'El Hombre en el umbral' [Man on the Threshold], called Christopher Dewey. This name is associated with that of John Dewey, the American philosopher and founder of 'instrumentalism', a theory maintaining that propositions are to be judged not by their truth but by their effectiveness. The intricate plot of the story is a brilliant illustration of this idea. In the story the truth that Dewey is seeking (to find out who killed the British judge) is said to be known by all: '*no hay un alma en esta ciudad que no sepa el secreto*' (*El aleph*, p. 145, emphasis in the original) [there's not a soul in this city (I suspected) who is not in on the secret (*Aleph*, p. 83)]. This 'secreto', however, turns out to be not an already existent account of a past assassination but a story which is made up and told to him to stall his enquiries while the real murder is actually being committed. By association the surname Dewey puns on the word 'instrumentalism' in that the story was not true, but effective; true, therefore, to its function: to be the 'instrument' to keep him from interfering with the crime.

Allusions encapsulating the plot element of a story

The fundamental place of paradox in the work of Borges needs no comment here. 'Los teólogos' [The Theologians], a story centred on a plot of oppositional rivalry concerns the paradox of the sameness of heresy and orthodoxy.[12] It is set in a cultural atmosphere redolent with gnosticism where to-day's orthodoxy is

---

[12]   See Mercedes Blanco's penetrating study of this story in 'Fiction historique et conte fantastique une lecture de "Los teólogos"', *Variaciones Borges*, vol. 4 (1997), pp 1-50

tomorrow's heresy. My interest in this story is to illustrate the way Borges manages to encapsulate the crux of the story (the interchangeability of values) into one richly allusive word, *Serpiente*. This is the name given to one of the heretical sects: 'la Cruz fue reemplazada por la Serpiente y la Rueda' (*El aleph*, p. 35) [The Wheel and the Serpent had displaced the Cross (*Labyrinths*, p. 150) and the fact that the following observations could be applied almost equally to either *cruz* or *rueda* only serves to emphasise further the motif of interchangeability. The serpent is a symbol present in most mythologies and religions with a variety of meanings. In Christianity, for instance, it is an emblem both of Christ and of some saints, as well as being the disguise of Lucifer as the tempter in the garden of Eden. In Gnostic mysticism, its cult occupies an important place and some sects derive their name from it, such as the Ophites (from the Greek *ophis*, snake), and the Nassenes (from the Hebrew *nahas*, also snake). This accurate historical precedent is disguised in 'Los teólogos' by the more transparent name, *serpiente*. Hans Jonas, in his wonderfully accessible introduction to *The gnostic religion* (1958) explains that in gnosticism traditional assumptions are turned on their head, so that whilst the biblical God is seen as a symbol of cosmic oppression, the serpent, through its action in the Garden of Eden, becomes the symbol of redemption. The serpent's deed in inducing Adam and Eve to disobey their creator and taste the fruit of knowledge is seen as something positive, marking the beginning of all *gnôsis* (knowledge) on earth. The name chosen by Borges therefore works on two levels: one, by conforming to historical precedent and two, by encapsulating through its own contradictory symbolism, the thematic underpinnings of the story of the indifferentiation between good and evil through paradox. But whereas there is in gnosticism, as in Cabala, some faith in that there is a *gnôsis*, a knowledge to be attained, even if through different and oppositional methods, a faith that 'if the riddle were solved it would reveal the immanent but hidden presence of the saviour principle within the world',[13] in Borges this solace is always presented ironically. In 'Los teólogos' paradox is not a riddle to be solved but a sign of meaninglessness. 'Aureliano supo que para la insondable divinidad, él y Juan de Panonia (el ortodoxo y el hereje, el aborrecedor y el aborrecido, el acusador y la víctima) formaban una sola persona' (*El aleph*, p. 45) [Aureliano learned that, for the unfathomable divinity, he and John of Pannonia (the orthodox believer and the heretic, the abhorrer and the abhorred, the accuser and the accused) formed one single person (*Labyrinths*, p. 158)]. The same downbeat cancellation of difference is reflected in the contradictoriness embodied in 'La Serpiente'.

Allusions which support the main metaphor of a story

There are many allusions in 'El aleph' which support the main conceit of the

---

[13]   See Bentley Layton, 'The riddle of the Thunder [NHC VI,2]. The Function of Paradox in a Gnostic Text from Nag Hammadi', in C.W. Hedrick and R. Hodgson, Jr (eds.), *Nag Hammadi Gnosticisms and Early Christianity* (Peabody, Mass : Hendrickson Publishers, 1986)

story in the form of a round disc acting as a microcosm of the universe and reflecting its variety. In a footnote towards the end of the story several fictional mirrors are listed which are said to have these same properties and it is rewarding to go to the original sources where these mirrors are described and find out the different emphases placed upon in each version: the mirror found by Tarik Benzayad showed the seven climates of the earth, Merlin's allowed King Ryence to see all and 'look into the hearts of men and foresee the intentions of his enemies and the treachery of his friends', whereas Luciano de Samosata's mirror allows one to hear everything and see the destinies of men, and Jupiter's sphere in Capella's *Satyricon* serves for Jupiter to mark 'those he wants to raise and those he wants to repress'. As each mirror claims to reveal the universal Truth, this concept is shown in its multiplicity, which is to say its vanity. Examples of 'universal poems' include Michael Drayton's *Polyolbion*, and the fictional and cruelly mocked *Canto Augural* or Canto Prologal, possibly a disparaging reference to Neruda's *Canto General*.[14] The shadow of Dante's *Commedia* is present throughout the story. Supporting this variety of allusions to universal microcosms is a reference to the world of sciences imperceptively contained in the story's title, 'El aleph'. According to the Cabala, the foremost meeting place of mathematics and mysticism, the world was created from the permutation of the 22 Hebrew letters, and, as Borges points out, the aleph, as the first letter of the Hebrew alphabet, enjoys a primacy which enables it to reflect all other letters. This renders it a perfect metaphor for a universal microcosm. But needless to say, the allusion to the aleph is 'unfaithful' (in Gracián's terms) in that Borges uses a 'sacred' concept ironically, for 'profane' ends. But what is of special interest here is not so much the idea that the revelation produced by the aleph in the story should be false, as the paradoxical suggestion that there exists not only one infinity but several. I have already hinted at this when I talked of the different 'universal' mirrors and 'universal' poems, but when Borges adds support from the *Mengenlehre* (set theory, of the German mathematician G. Cantor, 1829-1920) to his list, he moves into a different realm of metaphor.

The *Mengenlehre* is one of the most radical mathematical theories of the late ninteenth century. It is mentioned as yet another system dealing with the idea of infinity contained in the infinitesimal, but now giving the supposed reliability of mathematical support to the fiction. Cantor observed that the sequence 1,2,3,4, could equally be expressed as 2,4,6,8, or 2,4,6,8 squared or elevated to any power, so that 1 could be represented by 2, 2 by 4, 3 by 6, squared and elevated to any multiple power and so on. This makes any number in a series the potential representative of any other number, infinitely greater than itself; similarly 1 may be fragmented into a half, a third, or a 3018th and so on. This makes any cardinal number symbolic of any other, and of all others and, by extension, of infinitude; thus there are a host of potentially infinite numbers. This theory led Cantor to the paradoxical conclusion that the universe is

---

14   According to Emir Monegal, Borges disliked Neruda for his condemnation of the USA whilst remaining silent about Perón's dictatorship See *A Literary Biography*, pp 281-2

composed of an infinitude of points, as is a metre of the universe, or a fraction of that metre, making the most infinitesimal point on earth symbolic of the macrocosm. No doubt borrowing from the Cabala, Cantor actually uses the letter 'aleph' as an indicator of infinity, denoting a higher power than that of finite numbers, and discusses in the *Mengenlehre* a plurality of alephs.

The purpose of this brief foray into mathematics has not been to prove the influence of Cantor's theory on Borges's thinking but to point out the co-existence of the same metaphor in different and even supposedly opposite semantic fields and suggest that it is in the space created between these two contexts that new readings are forged. Not all of them are playful.

Allusions concerning the relationship of fantasy to reality

A striking example of the way in which some of Borges's fantasies seem to have a real cultural precedent is found in 'Tlön, Uqbar, Orbis, Tertius', with added piquancy because the realist example is used in a context of pure idealism. 'Tlön' is the imaginary realm to which the fiction of an imaginary country refers, and, concerned with the creation of an imaginary planet, a coherent fantasy safely discarded by the reader as a metaphor for an idealised alternative to our real world, that is, until hot, heavy, objects known as *hrönir* and *ur*, begin to invade the real planet much in the manner of science fiction. And yet, there was a historical precedent for what appears as the wildest fantasy, the corporality of the *hronır* resulting from belief in their existence. The argument runs roughly along the following lines: reading an article on the fictional Uqbar in a pirated copy of the tenth edition of the Encyclopedia Britannica, 'Borges' the narrator comes across a bibliographical reference to a clearly 'apocryphal' book entitled *Lesbare und lesenswerthe Bemerkungen über das Land Uqbar* allegedly by the seventeenth century satirist and theologian Johannes Valentinus Andreä. Some years later 'Borges' learns in Vol. 13 of De Quincey's *Writings* that whilst Andreä obviously did not write the aforementioned work, he might have done so since he did write a book about an imaginary community which was founded later, in imitation of what he had prefigured. De Quincy fleshes out this information with details that are relevant to 'Tlön' commenting that the reformist in Andreä, bent on redressing public morality, conceived a secret society of noble and learned men and claimed not only that the society was the repository of oriental mysteries, but also that it had been in existence for two hundred years. He was believed in his time and the non-existent society became the recipient of letters from all sorts of famous people, including Descartes. This non-existent community came into being through belief in its existence; from imaginary to real, Rosicrucianism became the subject of a massive literature, such that its bibliography took up 80 pages of Gardner's *Catalogue Raisonné of the Works on the Occult Sciences* (London 1903). The point that is here being made is that the fictional Encyclopedia of Tlön had a precedent in this legend which so invaded our reality that it created perhaps the first recorded *hron*, a hot, 'impressive' (in the literal sense) society and body of literature which in some way proceded to shape our history.

Intertextuality: interplay of meanings in 'La otra muerte'

By definition, allusions are to do with past texts, an important topic in 'La otra muerte' ['The Other Death']. This story is centred on several confused and contradictory versions of the death of Pedro Damian, said to have died of old age, as a deserter, but also as a young and brave hero in the battle of Masoller. The relationship between these two accounts or 'texts' is discussed with reference to a theological debate on God's ability (or inability) to undo the past. As mentioned in 'La otra muerte', this polemic ranged from Aristotle to Aquinas, both philosophers who maintain that God cannot undo the past, a view which is countered by the medieval ecclesiastic Pier Damiani (1007-72). Borges expands as follows: 'en el quinto capítulo de aquel tratado ('*De Omnipotentia*') sostiene contra Aristóteles y contra Fredegario de Tours, que Dios puede efectuar que no haya sido lo que alguna vez fué' (*El aleph*, p. 77) [in the fifth chapter of that treatise Pier Damiani asserts – against Aristóteles and Fredegarius de Tours – that it is within God's power to make what once was into something that has never been (*Aleph*, p. 70)]. If one looks up this reference in the mentioned fifth chapter of *De Omnipotentia* one finds that the argument springs from a statement by St. Jerome that virginity cannot be restored once lost through intercourse, an opinion Damiani refutes maintaining that God can make a woman a virgin again if she so dedicates herself to the spiritual life as to wipe out the *memory* of her previous actions (added emphasis). I should like to suggest that 'La otra muerte' is an æsthetic elaboration of this idea, based on Damiani's answer, namely, that history is made not by facts but by memories which can be 'corrected'. This would explain the co-existence of several supposed Universal histories represented in 'La otra muerte' by the different versions of Damian's death. But what is of immediate interest to this study of allusion is the intertextual relationship that has emerged between a story about valour (courage) and a debate on virginity. It is interesting though not surprising that Borges should have suppressed the more sensationalist aspect of this argument and yet directed the reader to it. The reward for pursuing the reference to its origin is to find a playful link between the desirability of heroic machismo and virginity.

However, there are further complications regarding the way the past is memorised. Damiani's explanation that God can undo the past if repentance is genuine may be set against the the opening lines of the story where the poem 'The Past' by Emerson is briefly mentioned. The American poet is known as a religious mystic, and is one the major exponents of the philosophy of Transcendentalism, yet if we follow the trail of the reference and read the poem in full we will find a fairly categorical statement that the Past is irrevocable: *not the gods can shake the past, nor the devil can finish what is packed/alter or mend eternal fact*. These lines, which stand in total contrast to the gist of 'La otra muerte', suggest a 'realist' counter-argument to the story, but, they, in turn, must be set against an opinion voiced later on in the story about Emerson which questions the authority of Emerson. When the character named Gannon was asked about the promised translation of the poem, he provocatively replied that he was not going to bother because 'la literatura española era tan tediosa que hacía innecesario a Emerson' (El aleph, p. 75) [Spanish literature is so boring it made Emerson quite superfluous (The Aleph and Other Stories, p. 51)]. Not only is it a classic put down by Borges of two targets with one stone, Emerson and Spanish literature, but it also serves as a disclaimer of Emerson's 'tedious' views. This is a perfect example of the way each allusion can problematise the previous one and its relationship to the story, adding shades of meaning to all interpretative intents. This destabilising exercise may be extended to the whole of Borges's output: for instance, in a (later) poem by Borges entitled 'Emerson', we find that thoughts attributed to him repeat Borges's own often expressed regrets, and subtly tie in with 'La otra muerte': 'Por todo el continente anda mi nombre; No he vivido. Quisiera ser otro hombre' (my emphasis) [The whole continent knows my name./ I have not lived. I want to be someone else.].[15] The wish to alter the past unites Borges with Emerson, with Pier Damiani and with his namesake, Pedro Damián.

Virginity and machismo are also strangely linked in 'El Sur'. In this story there is a passing reference which has received little attention so far but which if considered significant may add an ironic, not to say sentimental, touch to the death or 'suicide' of the central character. Dahlmann is about to engage in a duel which he does not want to fight and knows he will lose, but a sense of honour makes him go out and meet his certain death. His last thought before entering the fated almacén [general store] where he will be provoked, is of an engraving in an old edition of Paul et Virginie (1787), the well known sentimental story by Bernardin de St. Pierre. No further comment is given and the information is usually passed over or taken as providing some general atmosphere of bookishness. But there may be more: in the novel, the heroine Virginie chooses out of a sense of modesty and honour to die by drowning rather than undress and swim to safety. Attention to this allusion is rewarding in that it offers an interesting interpretative clue as an almost subliminal motivation for the decision taken by Dahlmann. Seen in this light it suggests a cycle of repeated deaths determined by cultural pressures. The demands of prudishness which affected Virginie are here translated to the demands of machismo which lead to Dahlmann's self sacrifice, two similar outcomes which, according to individual reader response, will be considered either a noble or a totally vain death.

In 'Pierre Menard, autor del Quijote' the reader is asked to imagine any text as if it were written by a variety of authors, in order to experience different readings ('la técnica del anacronismo deliberado y de las atribuciones erróneas') [the technique of deliberate anachronism and false attributions]. I seek shelter in this quotation, I am unfaithful to it, and with it I suggest new readings: that of

---

[15] Selected Poems (London. The Penguin Press, 1972), pp. 188-9 In the prologue to Discusión, Borges has famously stated 'Vida y muerte le han faltado a mi vida' [Life and death are missing from my life].

imagining any one of Borges's *Ficciones* as if it were a small kaleidoscope[16] in which new configurations are formed with every twist, according to which allusions are placed at the forefront.

---

[16]   The image comes from Schopenhauer and was used by Borges in *Other Inquisitions*, p. 58.

CHAPTER 5

Borges and the Plain Sense of Things

Gabriel Josipovici

The name Borges, among readers of modern literature, has always been synonymous with labyrinths, babelic libraries, gardens of forking paths, parallel universes, refutations of time and all sorts of cunning intellectual paradoxes. I want to argue, however, that these are merely the means whereby this profoundly modern writer seeks to make manifest the profound importance of the ordinary and the contingent in our lives and to remind us that this is the only life we have, that death will bring it to an end, and that every moment of it is infinitely precious. In this he is at one with Proust and Wallace Stevens, Beckett and Nabokov.

In saying this I am not saying anything particularly revolutionary. It is, after all, the message of one of Borges's greatest stories, the one he chose to place at the head of his finest collection, *Ficciones*, the story called 'Tlön, Uqbar, Orbis Tertius'.[1]

Let me remind you, briefly, how that story goes. With all the circumstantial detail that is the hallmark of his work, he describes, in the first person, how an alternative universe gradually encroached upon our own. It first enters his consciousness when his friend Bioy Casares refers in passing to the opinion of one of the heresiarchs of Uqbar, 'that mirrors and copulation are abominable, because they increase the number of men'. Asked by the narrator for the source of this, Bioy Casares mentions an encyclopedia entry on Uqbar, but when the two men look up the relevant volume they find no such entry. However, the next day a triumphant Bioy Casares calls him to say he has found it, at the end of volume XLVI of the encyclopedia he has at home, though the spine, which asserts that the contents run from Tor to Ups, makes no mention of Uqbar and the four pages on that country are found to figure in no other copy. Nor is there any reference to it in any of the atlases and travellers' accounts in the National Library. A short while later, however, Tlön and Uqbar manifest themselves to the narrator again, this time in the form of an entire volume found in a packet left in a bar, on his death, by a mysterious Englishman. This allows the narrator to put together rather more fully the history and intellectual ambience of that strange country.

Its culture is strictly idealist, and thus neither causality nor language as we know it exist: 'The world for them is not a concourse of objects in space; it is a heterogeneous series of independent acts. It is successive and temporal, not

---

[1]   Borges, *Ficciones* (Buenos Aires: Emecé, 1956)

spatial. There are no nouns in Tlön's conjectural *Ursprache* .... The perception of a cloud of smoke on the horizon and then of the burning field and then of the half-extinguished cigarette that produced the blaze is considered an example of association of ideas' (*Labyrinths*, pp. 32-4).[2]

Centuries of idealism 'have not failed to influence reality', the narrator goes on, in a nice double negative. 'In the most ancient regions of Tlön, the duplication of lost objects is not infrequent.' Two persons look for a pencil; the first finds it and says nothing; the second finds a second pencil, 'no less real, but closer to his expectations' (*Labyrinths*, pp. 37-8). These secondary objects are called *hrönir*, and these *hrönir* have little by little been ousting the real, banal objects, so that the world of Tlön is approximating more and more to the expectations of its inhabitants.

The rest of the story tells how this fantastic world has slowly invaded our own, helped on by a secret society dedicated to Tlön and its propagation. This society, we are told, is 'benevolent', and included George Berkeley among its founder members. At first there were only isolated examples of infiltration, but these gradually turned into a trickle. By 1944 the trickle has become an avalanche: 'Manuals, anthologies, summaries, literal versions, authorised re-editions and pirated editions of the Greatest Work of Man flooded and still flood the earth. Almost immediately, reality yielded on more than one account. The truth is that it longed to yield. Ten years ago any symmetry with a semblance of order – dialectical materialism, anti-Semitism, Nazism – was sufficient to entrance the minds of men. How could one do other than submit to Tlön, to the minute and vast evidence of an orderly planet?' Our world, it seems, will soon be indistinguishable from Tlön: 'Already the schools have been invaded by the (conjectural) "primitive language" of Tlön; already the teaching of its harmonious history (filled with moving episodes) has wiped out the one which governed my childhood; already a fictitious past occupies in our memories the place of another, a past of which we know nothing with certainty – not even that it is false .... If our forecasts are not in error, a hundred years from now ... English and French and mere Spanish will disappear from the globe. The world will be Tlön.'

At this point the narrator, who has not been much more that a literary device, suddenly takes centre stage: 'I pay no attention to all this', he writes, 'and go on revising, in the still days at the Adrogué hotel, an uncertain Quevedian translation (which I do not intend to publish) of Browne's *Urn Burial*' (*Labyrinths*, pp. 42-3).

It is easy enough to see the 'point' of the story: it is an anguished cry in the face of the persuasive ideologies which swept the world in the 1930s, and a kind of stoic refusal to submit to them. There is a puzzle about the dates: the story came out first in the collection *El jardín de senderos que se bifurcan* [The

---

[2]   Borges, *Labyrinths* (Harmondsworth· Penguin Books, 1970)

Garden of Forking Paths] in 1941, and was reprinted in the larger volume of 1944, *Ficciones* [Fictions]. Yet the latter part of the story is relegated to a postscript dated 1947. I presume this is a projection forward in time by the author writing in 1940 or 1941. He imagines then a world overtaken by Nazi ideology and dramatises what he would like his reaction to be: not so much passive resistance as a kind of quiet active resistance, the activity consisting of a completely selfless (he has no intention of publishing it) translation of a minor seventeenth-century prose work. The voluntary submission to a selfless task, to the carrying over into his native language of an author and a language far removed from him in space and intellectual interests, is the only way this quiet intellectual feels he can avoid being sucked into the idealist world of Tlön, that he can assert what he feels to be fundamental human values in a world rapidly turning into a mirror of our desires and imaginings.

It might be felt that the lumping together of 'dialectical materialism, anti-Semitism, Nazism' makes for a rather limp critique of the times, and that to see them all as one thing, and that thing an example of the idealist world of Tlön suggests a lack of political and historical acumen. Yet other stories – notably 'Deutsches Requiem' – as well as remarks he made in interviews, make it clear that the anglophile and democratic Borges was far from the uninvolved creator of private labyrinths he is often taken to be. On the other hand there is no doubt that the references to current events do seem rather perfunctory and that those stories, such as 'Deutsches Requiem', which deal with contemporary matters are not among his most successful. Indeed, one might say that they are among the least successful precisely because he assimilates a little too easily to his own concerns with the dangers of the imagination. It may be that Borges's mode of writing is not such as to engage fully with politics and history, like that of Sartre and Malraux: yet I would suggest that despite this his central contrast of the melancholy and resigned translator and the idealist world of Tlön is more deeply political than Malraux and Sartre can ever be, and that it helps to bring out something that is often overlooked in studies of literary modernism: that to write about politics without recognising the complicity of the forms of writing with the formation of political consciousness is to betray the cause one thinks one is serving, and that writers like Eliot, Stevens, Beckett and Borges may in the end be better guides to the times than Malraux, Sartre, Camus, Silone and the rest.

What then are the implications of the contrast between the narrator and the world of Tlön? And why, if Borges sees Tlön as a dangerous temptation and a fallacy, does he spend so much of his time and ingenuity in the construction of idealist universes? To answer this question it is necessary to understand the critique of traditional fiction that drives Borges's literary innovationism.

Let us go back to that burning cigarette: 'The perception of a cloud of smoke on the horizon and then of the burning field and then of the half-extinguished cigarette that produced the blaze is considered an example of association of ideas.' Not in the real world, we retort. But what of the world of fiction? After all, in that world there is no causality either, only the semblance of causality. For the smoke is not real smoke, the field not a real field and the cigarette not a real cigarette. The writer has put these three elements together in his mind and on paper and *we read it* as a story of how a fire was caused. Not a very interesting story, but a story nonetheless. The men of Tlön do not read it as a story but as an example of association of ideas. 'The world for them is not a concourse of objects in space; it is a heterogeneous series of independent acts' (*Labyrinths*, p. 32). In other words, the world of Tlön is the world of literature, shorn of its realist veneer.

We can now see why Borges is so fond of detective stories, and why detective stories should have emerged out of the crisis of Romanticism with the work of Poe. For detective stories go to the heart of the literary nature of literature and raise questions about the difference between causality in the real world and causality in the imagination: 'The Mysteries of the Rue Morgue' is the flip side of 'The Raven'.

Were we to find those three elements, the smoke on the horizon, the burning field, the half-extinguished cigarette, in a detective story the deduction that the cigarette caused the smoke on the horizon would figure as the first, obvious, banal explanation, later to be shown up by the detective to be false. It would have to be false because as it stands it is too obvious, too boring. No reader would bother with a writer of detective fiction who presented us with such a story and left it at that. Thus in Borges's story, 'Death and the Compass', the dull police inspector Treviranus, faced with a number of facts – a dead body in one hotel room, precious stones in the next room – comes up with the obvious explanation: 'No need to look for a three-legged cat here ... We all know that the Tetrarch of Galilee owns the finest sapphires in the world. Someone, intending to steal them, must have broken in here by mistake. Yarmolinsky got up: the robber had to kill him. How does that sound to you?' 'Possible, but not interesting', replies the detective hero, Lönnrot. 'You'll reply that reality hasn't the least obligation to be interesting. And I'll answer you that reality may avoid that obligation but that hypotheses may not. In the hypothesis you propose, chance intervenes, copiously. Here we have a dead rabbi; I would prefer a purely rabbinical explanation, not the imaginary mischances of an imaginary robber' (*Labyrinths*, p. 107).

Lönnrot, is of course, right. But his intuition leads to his own death, for the murderer is, in this story, one step ahead of the detective, has in fact produced an 'interesting' series of crimes precisely because he knows that Lönnrot has a weakness for the interesting. The ultimate victor, though, is the story: Borges has produced a classical detective tale with not one but two twists in the plot and only the most ingenious reader could have guessed the second one.

Borges's fondness for detective stories stems from his dislike for the classical novel. For the detective story accepts from the start that the logic of fiction is not the logic of life and that as a fictional construct its prime duty is to be interesting, not realistic. The novel, on the other hand, is a curious hybrid: it wants to assert at one and the same time that it is 'like life' in all its boring contingency, in its acceptance of scientific causality, while at the same time telling a story which implies that life has a meaning, is always more than mere contingency. That is the secret of its hold over us, as Sartre, for one, understood so well. We open a novel, says Sartre in *La Nausée*, and read about a man walking down a road. The man seems free, the future open before him. At once we identify with him, for that is how our own existence seems to be to us. We too are walking down the road of life, not knowing what is to come. But the pleasure of reading the novel lies in the fact that we know that this man is in fact the subject of an adventure that is about to befall him. How do we know this? Because he is there at the start of the novel and he would not be there if nothing were going to happen to him. Novels are precisely this: stories about the things that befall people. Thus, Sartre concludes, 'the end is there, which transforms everything. For us the guy is already the hero of the story'. The extraordinary power of the novel lies in this fact, that it makes us feel that our lives are both free *and* meaningful. It does not say this, for it neither needs to nor is even fully aware of it, but nonetheless that is its essence, the secret of its power.

Borges, like Beckett, dislikes the novel for two reasons, one having to do with literature and the other having to do with life. He dislikes it because he finds it tedious and uninteresting to imitate reality, and he dislikes it because he feels that it propagates a false view of life which stops us seeing what life is really like.

It is easy enough to understand the first reason: since literature is not tied to causality why not let the imagination roam free and discover its own rules and laws? But the way this is tied to the second is, despite the clarity of Sartre's analysis, rather more difficult to grasp. Let me turn briefly to another writer who may help us do so.

Sören Kierkegaard's great decade of writing took place exactly a hundred years before Borges's, in the years 1840-50. Nevertheless, the problems he was concerned with were almost identical to those of the Argentinian writer; but that should not deter us. Kierkegaard is concerned with what he calls 'actuality', with the stuff of life as it is lived, and with the way narratives about living, whether it be those of the novelists of his day or of a philosopher like Hegel, covertly falsify actuality. '"Actuality" cannot be conceived', he writes in his notebook for the year 1850. 'To conceive something is to dissolve actuality into *possibility* – but then it is impossible to conceive it, because conceiving something is transforming it into possibility and so not holding on to its actuality. As far as actuality is concerned, conception is retrogressive, a step backward, not a progress. Not that "actuality" contains no concepts, by no means; no, the concept which is come by through conceptually dissolving it into possibility is also inside actuality, but there is still something more – that is actuality. To go from possibility to actuality is a step forward ...; to go from actuality to possibility is a step backward. But there's this deplorable confusion in that modern times have incorporated "actuality" into logic and then, in distraction, forgotten that "actuality" in logic is still only a "thought actuality", i.e. it is possibility.'

Everything would be fine if works of fiction and works like Hegel's *Phenomenology* presented themselves as hypotheses, but they do not. They present themselves as actuality. And it is the same with history. 'But isn't history actual? Certainly. But what history? No doubt the six thousand years of the world's history are actuality, but one that is put behind us; it is and can exist for me only as thought actuality, i.e. as possibility. Whether or not the dead have actually realised existentially the tasks which were put before them in actuality has now been decided, has been concluded; there is no more existential actuality for them except in what has been put behind them, which again, for me, exists only as ideal actuality, as thought actuality, as possibility.'[3]

I can think of history as actuality, but the very thinking robs it of its actuality. If I am to grasp the actual I have somehow to think against thinking, to imagine against the imagination. Already in 1837 – before, that is, he had published any of his books – Kierkegaard had struggled to make sense of this conundrum. He had done so by drawing a contrast between the indicative, the mode of actuality, and the subjunctive, the mode of possibility: 'The indicative thinks something as actual (the identity of thinking and the actual). The subjunctive thinks something as thinkable.' The writer sensitive to the gulf between thinking and living will reflect this distinction by choosing the subjunctive, not the indicative. 'One should be able to write a whole novel in which the present tense subjunctive was the invisible soul, as light is for painting' (*ibid.*, p. 91).

The true writer, conscious of the nature of the actual, will use the subjunctive precisely because the indicative means so much to him: 'This is why one can truthfully say that the subjunctive, which enters a glimpse of the individuality of the person in question, is a dramatic line whereby the narrator steps aside and makes the remark as being true of the character (poetically), not as factual, not even as if it might be fact: it is presented under the illumination of subjectivity' (*ibid.*, p. 91).

This helps to explains why so many modern writers have been at pains to stress that their fictions are only fictions, not reality. This is not in order to play games with the reader or to deny the world but on the contrary, out of a deep sense of the wondrous nature of the world and a determination not to confuse the world as it is with the world as we imagine it to be. Borges is quite clear about this in both the parable and the poem he has devoted to the tiger. 'Never can my dreams engender the wild beast I long for', he writes in the prose piece. 'The tiger indeed appears, but stuffed or flimsy, or with impure variations of shape, or of an implausible size, or all too fleeting, or with a touch of the dog or the bird.'

[3]   Sören Kierkegaard, *Papers and Journals A Selection*, ed. and trans. Alastair Hannay (Harmondsworth Penguin Books, 1996), p 470

And the poem ends by directing us away from poetry to the living beast: 'I go on/ Seeking through the afternoon time/ The other tiger, that which is not in verse.' In his stories he invents plots that help to bring out the contrast between the indicative and the subjunctive: the man who waits for his killers to come, imagining again and again the moment of their arrival, until he can no longer distinguish the reality from his nightmares; the creature lost in the labyrinth of his melancholy life, welcoming with relief the coming of Theseus, who will put an end to his solitude; the Symbolist writer who refuses the pleasures of mere imagination and sets out to write that which is quite other than any of our imaginings. As with Beckett and Stevens, Borges's imagination keeps trying to imagine the death of imagination, but it is only when the imagination has been given its head that it can be effectively exorcised and so allow actuality to shine through.

For imagination to be exorcised it must be released from the constraints of the causality that operates in the real world; by so doing it will make clear what realistic fiction obscures, drive a wedge between imagination and reality. 'In spite of having been a child in a symmetrical garden of Hai Feng, was I – now – going to die?' asks the Chinese agent in 'The Garden of Forking Paths' (*Labyrinths*, p. 45), and the story is designed to bring him – and us – to understanding of what that 'now' means.

First of all we must be weaned from our lack of curiosity about 'nowness', from our taking it for granted. To do so we must be made to realise how very strange it is that everything that happens to us happens, precisely, now. And this can be done by making us grasp that things *could have been otherwise but were not*. 'In all fictional worlds', Stephen Albert, the sinologist, explains to the Chinese agent, 'each time a man is confronted with several alternatives, he chooses one and eliminates the others; in the fictional of Ts'ui Pên, he chooses – simultaneously – all of them. He *creates*, in this way, diverse futures, diverse times which themselves also proliferate and fork. Here, then, is the explanation of the novel's contradictions. Fang, let us say, has a secret; a stranger calls at his door; Fang resolves to kill him. Naturally, the intruder can kill Fang, they both can escape, they both can die, and so forth. In the work of Ts'ui Pên, all possible outcomes occur; each one is the point of departure for other forkings. Sometimes the paths of this labyrinth converge: for example, you arrive at this house, but in one of the possible pasts you are my enemy, in another, my friend ... '(see *Labyrinths*, p. 53).

The traditional novel, by refusing to countenance the fact that things could have been otherwise stops us also from understanding the strangeness of the fact that they are not otherwise, but thus. 'Thus', 'now', can never be written, for that would turn them from actuality again into possibility. 'Now' can only be pointed to, not uttered. 'In a riddle whose answer is chess', Stephen Albert asks the Chinese agent, 'what is the only prohibited word?' 'I thought a moment and replied: "The word chess".' The classic novel, unaware of its complicity with the forces of falsehood, imagining that it deals with actuality when it deals only with possibility, blithely includes such words in its discourse. The more fastidious writer, aware of what he is doing, knows that his only way of conveying the sense of the word is to construct a riddle or labyrinth whose answer is the missing word. He cannot speak the word, for that will destroy it; he must not even succumb to the temptation to look for a superior language in which that word might exist. That is the crime of the Chinese agent, who, realising that his human voice is 'weak' and cannot rise above 'the uproar of the war', decides that the only way to send his message to Germany is to murder a man. 'I have won out abominably', he concludes. 'I have communicated to Berlin the secret of the city they must attack ... The Chief has deciphered this mystery. He knew my problem was to indicate (through the uproar of the war) the city called Albert, and that I had found no other means to do so than to kill a man of that name. He does not know (no one can know) my innumerable contrition and weariness' (*Labyrinths*, p. 54).

What is the missing word of 'Tlön, Uqbar, Orbis Tertius'? The answer is 'the actual', what Wallace Stevens called 'the plain sense of things'. A conventional narrative would, like mirrors and copulation, merely double our confusion; Borges's narrative, recognising that 'the absence of the imagination had/ Itself to be imagined', manages to convey the 'nowness', the 'thusness' of actuality, to which the narrator commits himself at the end. There is no better gloss on it, and on all Borges's work, than Stevens's poem actually called 'The Plain Sense of Things':

> After the leaves have fallen, we return
> To a plain sense of things. It is as if
> We had come to an end of the imagination,
> Inanimate in an inert savoir.
> It is difficult even to choose the adjective
> For this blank cold, this sadness without cause.
> The great structure has become a minor house.
> No turban walks across the lessened floors.
>
> . . . .
>
> Yet the absence of the imagination had
> Itself to be imagined. The great pond,
> The plain sense of it, without reflections, leaves,
> mud, water like dirty glass, expressing silence
>
> Of a sort, silence of a rat come out to see
> The great pond and its waste of lilies, all this
> Had to be imagined as an inevitable knowledge,
> Required, as a necessity requires.

CHAPTER 6

Jorge Luis Borges and the European Avant-Garde

Jason Wilson

'Borges dejó de ser ultraísta a partir del primer verso ultraísta que escribió'
Néstor Ibarra
[Borges stopped being an ultraist from the first ultraist line that he wrote]

'European avant-garde' is a misnomer. Borges cunningly disregarded the Paris-based avant-garde of the first thirty years of this century adopted by most Latin Americans of his generation in favour of Anglo-American, Spanish and German versions. In an essay in *Inquisiciones* he opposed 'la afrancesada secta de voces ... de quienes se dedican a vocear nubes y a gesticular balbuceos' [the Frenchified sect of voices of those who dedicate themselves to shout clouds and gesticulate babblings],[1] clearly dismissing Baudelaire ('nubes') and the surrealists ('balbuceos'). Borges recalled the days of the magazine *Martín Fierro*: 'Me disgustaba lo que representaba, que era la idea francesa de que la literatura se renueva permanentemente, que Adán renace cada mañana, y también la idea de que como París tiene cenáculos que se revuelcan en la publicidad y en la discusión ociosa, nosotros debíamos adecuarnos a los tiempos' [What they stood for annoyed me, which was the French idea that literature renews itself continuously, that Adam is born every morning and also the idea that as Paris has literary groups that wallow in publicity and leisurely arguments, we should adapt to the times].[2] In 1927 the Peruvian poet César Vallejo did not grasp this odd strategy, and in his essay 'Contra el secreto profesional' [Against the professional secret] accused Borges of lacking 'honestidad espiritual' [mental honesty], of being rhetorical, impotently creating a 'literatura prestada' [borrowed literature], mimicking the latest European avant-garde. Jorge Luis Borges simply mirrored Ribemont-Dessaignes. Vallejo characterised Borges as exercising 'un fervor bonaerense tan falso y epidérmico como lo es ... el cosmopolitismo a la moda de todos los muchachos americanos de última hora' [a Buenos Aires fervour as false and as superficial as the trendy cosmopolitanism of all the South American boys of the latest promotion].[3] Vallejo had singled Borges out both as an *ultraísta* (the weak, mimetic, Hispanic version of the avant-garde), as well as the poet of *Fervor de Buenos Aires* (1923), where the earlier metaphoric excesses had been pruned.

[1]   *Inquisiciones* [1925] (Buenos Aires Seix Barral, 1994), p, 163. Translations are mine unless otherwise indicated
[2]   'Las memorias de Borges', *La Opinión*, 17 de setiembre de 1974, pp. I-XXIII, quote from p. XIV
[3]   César Vallejo, *Literatura y arte* (Buenos Aires Ediciones de Mediodía, 1966), pp. 33-9

Borges's eight years in Europe had given him a close view of what was happening. He translated German Expressionist poetry, met and admired the Spaniards Rafael Cansinos Asséns and Ramón Gómez de la Serna, and published 'daring' poems in the new mode in Spanish periodicals like *Cervantes, Grecia* and *Ultra.* Borges brought these adventures back to Buenos Aires, and participated in the movement against the influence of Rubén Darío ('simulacros de Rubén ... infectaban las prensas' [simulacrums of Rubén ... infected the presses],[4] in favour of metaphor and a local Argentine slant that would link Borges with other experimentalists like Oliveiro Girondo and Ricardo Güiraldes in a literary activity that centred on magazines like *Proa* and *Martín Fierro.* In these poems the *calle*, with its contemporary tram music, its *zozobra* and *vértigo,* made Borges feel modern, against the *abuelos*, where walking the streets transformed him into a poet-*flâneur.* All this *porteño* bustle has been well summarised by Beatriz Sarlo.[5]

Borges opted for Hispanic, Germanic and Anglo-American modernism, and denigrated Paris-based Dada, and then Surrealism,[6] assuming that writing a poem was an aesthetic act that took place on a page and in the mind, *el puro goce estético [pure aesthetic thrill].*[7] Turning a deaf ear to the relationship of the poet to his times was crucial in Borges's later self-definition, despite writing early poems praising the 1917 Russian Revolution.

The Parisian avant-garde, as we know, was always militant. By 1916 Dada was undermining the status of the poem in terms of its humanistic intentions. André Breton's surrealism opened out this quarrel about the poem by arguing that literature had to merge with revolution to bring about a more fulfilling reality (surreality), and change both society and the poet in a clearly extra-literary and political way. By 1926 Breton had joined the French Communist Party; in 1935 he linked quotations from Marx and Rimbaud, claiming that only a revolution could justify art by changing man and life ('"Transformer le monde", a dit Marx; "Changer la vie", a dit Rimbaud: ces deux mots d'ordre pour nous n'en font qu'un' ["Transform the world", said Marx; "Change life", said Rimbaud: these two words of order for us are but one].[8]

Borges deliberately ignored this radical option facing European artists after the first world war. Despite lip-service to the 1917 Revolution, a poetics of revolutionary change did not excite his imagination. He did not share Breton's enthusiasm for the surrealist tradition as outlined in the first surrealist manifesto

---

[4]   *Inquisiciones*, p 29

[5]   Beatriz Sarlo, *Jorge Luis Borges A Writer on the Edge* (London & New York: Verso, 1993)

[6]   There are no references to Surrealism in Evelyn Fishburn and Psyche Hughes, *A Dictionary of Borges* (London Duckworth, 1996), or in D Balderston, *The Literary Universe of Jorge Luis Borges An Index to References and Allusions to Persons, Titles and Places in His Writings* (New York Greenwood, 1986)

[7]   *Textos cautivos Ensayos y reseñas en 'El Hogar' 1936-1939*, edition of Enrique Sacerio-Garí & Emir Rodríguez Monegal (Barcelona Tusquets, 1986), p 148

[8]   André Breton, *Manifestes du Surréalisme* (Paris· Jean-Jacques Pauvert, 1962), p 285.

in 1924 linking poetry with rebellion against the jaded world the young surrealists found themselves in. Borges restricted the action of the poem to rebelling against earlier poets like Darío and 'la vigente lugonería' [the current Lugonese].[9] Being modern meant shrinking the poem to clever metaphors ('metaforicé con fervor' [I metaphoricised with fervour],[10] like the Anglo-American Imagists; it meant shunning direct colloquial language by applying a system of outrageous synonyms that he called baroque. A poem avoided that radical self-evaluation proposed by creative early readings of Freud. Borges was not alone in this blending of aesthetics with an apparent novelty, for he shared his mode of writing with the Hispanic avant-garde in general, who took this route (as noted by Vallejo), following the lead of Vicente Huidobro, and barely disguising Juan Ramón Jiménez's notion of *poesía pura* where the poem itself became the ultimate meditative experience.

The avant-garde for Borges was simply a matter of a new style, not a grappling with contemporary anguish, nor a transgression of limits, nor a quest for freedom. *Ultraísmo* was a confused off-shoot of the European avant-garde, with Hispanic poets playing at being modern with the new algebra of metaphors (Ortega y Gasset's phrase) and lexical references to modernity like, in Borges's words, 'el avión, las antenas y la hélice' [aeroplane, aerials, propeller];[11] in fact just being different to their immediate predecessors. Later Borges famously confessed that the Argentine avant-garde came out of Lugones's 1909 collection *Lunario sentimental* ('descubrir las metáforas que Lugones ya había descubierto' [to discover the metaphors that Lugones had already discovered].[12] No wonder Borges refused to collect his *ultraísta* writings because he had not worked out how to insert himself into a poetic tradition which opposed aesthetics by committing itself to the nightmare and contingencies of history. Against his baroque extravaganzas Borges would assert the limitations of his experiences, a kind of honesty at odds with all versions of Romantic glamour. Accepting the inheritance of the Hispanic tradition that claimed the poem as an aesthetic space authenticated by the poet's sincerity, Borges was condemned to being a speculative poet (generated by verbs like *reflexionar, pensar*) of inner life and formative, eccentric readings. In his poem 'Baltasar Gracián' he wrote what appeared to be a critique of Spanish Golden Age speculative poetry: 'Laberintos, retruécanos, emblemas / Helada y laboriosa nadería, / Fue para este jesuita la poesía, / Reducida por él a estratagemas. / No hubo música en su alma, sólo un vano / Herbario de metáforas y argucias' [Labyrinths, puns, emblems/ Frozen and laborious nothings/ was what poetry was to this Jesuit/ reduced by him to stratagems. / There was no music in his soul, only a vain / herbarium of metaphors and sophistry].[13] Much later, Borges confessed that this poem 'makes

---

[9]   *El tamaño de mi esperanza* [1926] (Buenos Aires· Seix Barral, 1993), p 70.

[10]   Miguel de Torre (recop), *Borges Fotografías y manuscritos* (Buenos Aires.Ediciones Renglón, 1987), p 74

[11]   *Inquisiciones*, p. 105.

[12]   Jorge Luis Borges, *Obra poética* (Madrid/Buenos Aires: Emecé, 1972), p. 9.

[13]   *Ibid*, p. 143

fun of me. I am the Gracián of that poem'.[14] In the prologue to *La cifra*, Borges modestly defined his poetry as 'intelectual'.[15] This crisis about what a poem really meant led Borges into a silent desperation, almost a poet's block, for between 1929 and 1960 he published only twenty-one new poems. He knew that he was out of tune with his times, and that his anachronistic poems were sincere but private artefacts written in direct speech, avoiding the baroque. In 1969 Borges wrote: 'Es curiosa la suerte del escritor. Al principio es barroco, vanidosamente barroco, y al cabo de los años puede lograr ... no la sencillez que no es nada, sino la modesta y secreta complejidad' [The fate of the writer is curious. At first it's baroque, conceitedly baroque, and after years he can attain, not simplicity which is nothing, but a modest and secret complexity].[16] As a poet Borges had dropped out of history, confusing baroque with avant-garde, as if he had taken Antonio Machado's rage against the Spanish baroque ('pura agudeza verbal' [pure verbal wit][17] as a sign not to publish poems (Borges had dreamed of being 'un escritor español del siglo diecisiete' [a Spanish eighteenth century writer] and later lamented in his strange English 'I wallowed in newfangled words'). Given Borges's admiration for Antonio Machado it is tempting to link Machado's scorn for the surrealists as 'mulas de noria' [waterwheel mules],[18] his dismissal of Huidobro's metaphors as empty and heartless and the realist novel as annoyingly packed with stupid anecdotes, insignificant details, and lacking 'toda elaboración imaginativa, reflexiva, estética' [all imaginative, thoughtful and aesthetic elaboration][19] as stimulants to Borges's own views.

Why Borges misread the radical French tradition embodied in Rimbaud, Lautréamont, Dada and Surrealism is hard to explain; there are personal reasons (his quirky readings, his cunning poetic temperament; what I call his aesthetics of timidity); geographic ones (he lived in Switzerland – Geneva, not Zurich, so missed out on Dada's café Voltaire – then Lugano, Mallorca and Spain), but mainly cultural (he was not European, unaffected by the trauma of the Great War; he opted for the tepid Hispanic, Germanic and Anglo-American modernisms).

To investigate Borges's retreat into a poetic stasis I will briefly outline his aversion to surrealism and argue that he defined himself against some key Parisian avant-garde terms. Beatriz Sarlo noted that 'the order of his fantasy has nothing in common with the surrealist imagination'[20] and that Borges practically ignored the movement, yet Borges published in Emile Malaspine's magazine *Manomètre*, alongside Péret, Soupault and Tzara, even though, in Salas's words 'el peso teórico del surrealismo sobre el conjunto de su obra fuera nulo' [the

---

[14]   Carlos Cortínez (ed), *Borges the Poet* (Fayetteville University of Arkansas Press, 1986), p 43.

[15]   *La cifra* (Madrid· Alianza Editorial, 1981), p 11

[16]   Borges, *Obra poética*, p 114

[17]   Antonio Machado, *Obras Poesía y prosa* (Buenos Aires Losada, 1974), p. 345

[18]   *Ibíd* , p 569

[19]   *Ibíd* , p 498

[20]   Sarlo, *Jorge Luis Borges*, p. 53

theoretical weight of surrealism on the bulk of his work was nil][21]. I will argue
the opposite; that his distaste for surrealism defined his later poetics.

For Borges all surrealist poetry was just a 'coquetería' [flirtatiousness][22]
where the poets pretended to write incoherently (his critique of automatic
writing?). Borges defined experimental writing in 1937 as 'simular el desorden,
construir difícilmente un caos, usar la inteligencia para obtener los efectos de la
casualidad' [to fake disorder, to construct a chaos with difficulties, to use
intelligence to obtain the effects of chance], quoting Mallarmé, James Joyce, and
Ezra Pound as figures in that 'extraña tradición' [strange tradition].[23] In 1945
Borges made his antipathy obvious when praising Paul Valéry's lucidity in an
'era bajamente romántica, en la era ... de la secta de Freud y de los comerciantes
del *surréalisme*' [basely romantic period, in a period of Freud's sect and the
traders in surrealism].[24]

In 1938 Borges reviewed the manifesto André Breton signed with Diego
Rivera in Mexico (though Borges had no idea it was actually written by Trotsky,
Diego Rivera's house guest in Coyoacán). Borges's hostility to the idea of a
collective manifesto is obvious from the first line when he said that 20 years
back manifestos 'pululaban' [infested].[25] Borges then summarised the kind of
manifestos that he was involved in through his *ultraísta* activities, with their
purely literary recommendations (abolish punctuation and rhyme in favour of
metaphors etc). These manifestos were 'charlatanes' [gossipy], but innocuous,
and now 'superados' [superceded] in charlatanry by Breton's. He called
Breton's and Rivera's document 'increíble' [unbelievable], 'precipitado' [hasty],
written 'con terquedad' [with stubbornness]. Three thousand words to say two
contradictory things. The first is that art should be free, which Borges mocks as
worthy of Perogrullo [Platitude]. Ignoring Breton's lucid anti-Stalinist stance,
Borges added: 'Es absurdo que el arte sea un departamento de la política' [It's
absurd that art should be a branch of politics].[26] Borges cited what he found most
ridiculous: Breton's attack on 'indiferentismo político' [political indifference]
and that 'la tarea suprema del arte contemporáneo es participar consciente y
activamente en la preparación de la revolución' [the supreme task of
contemporary art is to participate consciously and actively in preparing for a
revolution].[27] Borges ended ironically defending his individualistic, apolitical
view of the artist: 'Pobre arte independiente el que premeditan, subordinado a
pedanterías de comité y a cinco mayúsculas' [Poor independent art premeditated
by them, subordinated to pedantries of a committee and five capital letters], the
last a reference to F.I.A.R.I. (Fédération Internationale de l'Art Révolutionnaire

---

[21]   Horacio Salas, *Borges   Una biografía* (Buenos Aires: Planeta, 1994), p. 105.

[22]   *Textos cautivos* , p 173

[23]   *Ibid* , p 173

[24]   Borges, *Obras completas* (Buenos Aires: Emecé, 1974), p 687

[25]   *Textos cautivos*, p 288

[26]   *Ibid* , p. 288

[27]   *Ibid* , p 288

Indépendant) the organisation that Breton set up in Paris on return from Mexico in 1938. In 1974 Borges claimed in a conversation with Ferrari that German Expressionism was 'superior a otras escuelas contemporáneas (como ... Surrealismo)' [superior to other contemporary schools, such as surrealism];[28] in 1985 that German Expressionism was 'mucho más interesante que el superrealismo' [far more interesting than surrealism].

I want now to look at the notion of revolutionary change. In 1920 and 1921Borges published three poems praising Lenin's 1917 triumph in Moscow, 'Rusia' [Russia], 'Gesta maximalista' [Maximum Deed], and 'Guardia roja' [Red Guard] in the lit-mags *Grecia, Ultra* and *Tableros*.[29] He never collected them, but planned a volume called *Los himnos rojos* or *Los ritmos rojos [Red Hymns, Red Rhythms]* as told in his 'memorias' in 1974: 'Era una colección de poemas – quizás veinte – en verso libre en alabanza de la Revolución Rusa. ... Este libro lo destruí en vísperas de mi partida' [It was a collection of perhaps twenty poems in free verse praising the Russian revolution ..... I destroyed the book on the eve of my departure].[30] 'Rusia' ends with a panegyric: 'Clamaremos su gesta / bayonetas / que portan en la punta las mañanas' [Let us proclaim its epic/ bayonets / that carry morning on their tips]; the revolution as metaphor of the dawn of the new technological century. Borges's poetics is grounded on *le nouveau*, identifying himself with this new future. The rest of the poem is an excuse for metaphorising in Huidobro's *creacionista* way. The 'arco iris' [rainbow] becomes a 'cuerno salvaje' [wild horn]; 'mediodías' [middays] explode in eyes, and, derivatively Huidobran, the sun is 'crucified'. The poem 'Gesta maximalista' has rifles as viaducts; red flags as birds, barricades as scars along the squares and inner solstices burning out the skull. The line 'vibran nervios desnudos' [naked nerves vibrate], catching the new energy, recalls Huidobro's 'Arte poética' of 1916 directly: 'y el alma del oyente quede temblando' [and the soul of the listener will remain trembling], and 'estamos en el ciclo de los nervios' [we are in the cycle of the nerves]. Reality is too easily displaced by verbal images; Borges's is a playful, fun revolution, emptied of political or personal involvement. Later Borges would find Huidobro abusive, pointlessly chasing metaphors he never found, a player of games.[31]

Much as André Breton also characterised surrealist imagery in his first surrealist manifesto, it is what the surrealists intended that really engaged him. The only way to live poetry was to adopt a '*non-conformisme* absolu',[32] and fight for freedom ('Le seul mot de liberté est tout ce qui m'exalte encore' [The single word freedom is the only one that still exalts me],[33] with automatic writing as a means of liberating the predictable, literal, conscious mind 'en

---

28 *Obras completas*, p 126

29 Cited in Salas, *Borges Una biografía*, p 70

30 'Las memorias de Borges', p. IX.

31 *Obras completas*, p 32.

32 Breton, *Manifestes du Surréalisme*, p 40.

33 *Ibid*, p 17

dehors de toute préoccupation esthétique ou morale' [outside all aesthetic or moral preoccupations],[34] with a 'louable mépris de ce qui pourrait s'ensuivre littérairement' [praiseworthy scorn of all that could follow in a literary sense]. There is no need to dwell on Breton's scorn for literature in favour of a 'comportement lyrique' [lyrical behaviour],[35] the process of writing, the kick of inspiration, and writing as a journey ('descente vertigineuse') into the psyche. The contrast with Borges is glaring. The surrealists flirted more and more openly with revolution, even denigrating the surrealist revolution in the title of their second magazine *Le Surréalisme au Service de la Révolution* (July, 1930) until the group splintered over French Communist Party membership in the late 1920s. Over this same period Borges distanced himself completely from any notion of revolutionary change. Borges's nihilism, the *nada* behind personality, and the invasion of the reader by the author are his passive responses to Bretonian change.

The second crucial term in surrealism that entranced Breton was the 'dream' ('le rêve ne peut-il être appliqué ... à la résolution des questions fondamentales de la vie' [Cannot the dream be applied to resolve life's basic questions]).[36] Freud's *The Interpretation of Dreams* (1900) offered the surrealists the famous royal road to the unconscious, beyond common sense and rational scrutiny. Freud's dream as a disguised fulfilment of repressed wishes led Breton to postulate that the dream was in fact a metaphor of freedom ('Tue, vole plus vite, aime tant qu'il te plaira' [kill, fly faster, love as much as you want]),[37] with the unconscious a wonderland where *le merveilleux* simply waited to burst out. The aim was to liberate *la pensée* in order to feel completely alive. To be a poet meant breaking taboos, transgressing the social codes, exploring the psychic theatre. Surrealism simply wanted people to live their dreams ('rentrer le rêve dans son véritable cadre ... la vie de l'homme' [to return the dream into its true framework]).[38] Unlike Freud, Breton believed in *pleine satisfaction*.

Borges was equally fascinated by dreams, but detested Freud ('un homme aux prises avec une obsession sexuelle' [a man gripped by a sexual obsession)[39]. Borges's view of the dream was purely 'manifest', all surface, a puzzling narrative. He called Poe's and Kafka's stories 'pesadillas' [nightmares],[40] as if faithfully reproducing the realism of a dreamscape. To dream, to day-dream, became synonyms for the work of art, for reading, for speculating; dreaming is a 'género literario' [literary genre][41] that follows aesthetic and dramatic laws, an enigmatic source of writing, as Borges wrote in his poem 'El sueño' [the dream]:

---

[34]   *Ibid* , p. 37

[35]   *Ibid* , p. 62

[36]   *Ibid.*, p 25.

[37]   *Ibid* , p. 26.

[38]   *Ibid* , p. 27.

[39]   Emir Rodríguez Monegal, *Borgès par lui-même* (Paris: Editions Seuil, 1970), p. 91.

[40]   Borges, *Obra Poética*, p 225. 'Textos cautivos', p. 121.

[41]   Osvaldo Ferrari, *Borges en diálogo* (Buenos Aires: Grijalbo, 1985), p 171.

'De esa región rescato restos / que no acabo de comprender' [From that region I rescue remains / that I never manage to understand].[42] Literature is a 'sueño dirigido' [directed dream].[43] Commenting on this last quotation José Miguel Oviedo wrote 'It's not that he is subscribing, of course, to the Surrealist theory of automatic writing, but underscoring the idea that the writer is only the partial author of a work ...'[44]

Rimbaud's battle call – 'Il faut être absolument moderne' [One must be absolutely modern][45] – rallied all the different expressions of Parisian avant-garde activity. To be modern meant to subvert tradition in terms of a utopian impulse; it meant more than being fashionable. It was political, shocking, daring. Surrealism exploited Rimbaud's '*dérèglement de tous les sens*' [derangement of all the senses] in order to reach '*l'inconnu*' [the unknown],[46] where the unknown was equated with free-floating desire.

However Borges may have felt the thrill of being modern in the 1920s ('Soy el primer aventurero hispánico que ha arribado al libro de Joyce...' [I am the first Hispanic adventurer who has arrived at Joyce's book])[47] he soon turned his back on the dangers and risks of avant-garde poetry by confusing it with baroque over-writing, with being rhetorical and insincere. He later justified his change by stating in 1937: 'tuvimos el arrojo de ser hombres de nuestro tiempo como si la contemporaneidad fuera un acto difícil y voluntarioso y no un rasgo fatal' [We dared to be men of our time, as if being contemporaneous was a difficult, wilful act and not a fateful trait].[48] He repeated this point in 1969: 'Hacia 1905 Hermann Bahr decidió: El único deber, ser moderno. Veintitantos años después, yo me impuse también esa obligación del todo superflua. Ser moderno es ser contemporáneo, ser actual; todos fatalmente lo somos' [Towards 1905 Hermann Bahr decided: The only duty, to be modern. Twenty something years later, I also imposed this obligation on myself in a completely superflous way. To be modern is to be contemporaneous, to be up to date; we are all fated to be so].[49] By denying militant Paris-based modernism, Borges retreated into an essentialist aesthetic where time and change appeared not to matter.

Borges has always mocked the novel for its padding, its length ('Desvarío laborioso y empobrecedor el de componer vastos libros...' [A laborious and impoverishing whim that of composing vast books]), despite reading and commenting on numerous novelists, admiring Virginia Woolf, and especially Faulkner and Conrad. In his early essay on Joyce's *Ulysses* Borges admitted that

---

42   Borges, *La rosa profunda* (Buenos Aires: Emecé, 1985), p. 21.

43   Borges, *Obras completas,* p 1022

44   In Cortínez, *Borges the Poet,* p. 127.

45   Arthur Rimbaud, *Oeuvres Complètes* (Paris· Gallimard, 1972), p 116

46   *Ibid* , p. 251.

47   *Obras completas,* p. 23

48   '*Textos cautivos,* p 98.

49   *Obra poética,* p 59.

he had not read all the 700 pages ('Confieso haberlo practicado solamente a retazos' [I confess that I practised it only in bits and pieces]).[50] In a 1939 note on Joyce's *Work in Progress* Borges revealed how he read novels: 'En el *Ulysses* hay sentencias, hay párrafos, que no son inferiores a los más ilustres de Shakespeare ... En el mismo *Finnegan's Wake* hay alguna frase memorable' [In *Ulysses* there are maxims, there are paragraphs that are not inferior to Shakespeare's most famous ones. Even in *Finnegan's Wake* there are memorable sentences].[51] Borges read Joyce's prose for its odd memorable lines where the magic of language touched him. This follows Poe's dictum that 'what we term a long poem is, in fact, merely a succession of brief ones', a way of reading that assumes that the short-lived intensity of concentration breaks all literature up into lyrical fragments. Borges once admitted that he had never finished Güiraldes's novel *Don Segundo Sombra*.[52] Borges's view of the novel seems to agree with Breton's. However, Breton attacked what he called false realism, Paul Valéry's arbitrary snippet of information *la marquise sortit à cinq heures*. Milan Kundera recently summarised Breton's objections: 'data; description; pointless attention to the null moments of existence; a psychology that makes the character's every move predictable; in short ... the fatal lack of poetry'.[53] Both Breton and Borges sought the poetry buried behind the verbiage of the realist novel; but what this poetry was separated them. Borges once divided poetry into two kinds; the one he preferred after his dismissal of *ultraísmo* was classical, atemporal, aesthetic, based on *limpidez* (clear language) and *temblor* (aesthetic emotion) while the avant-garde – surrealism – sought 'la invención escandalosa y el experimento cargado de porvenir' [scandalous invention and experiments loaded with future],[54] as if those two concepts fell outside the arena of literature. All avant-garde poetry ends up as 'mero escándalo' [mere scandal],[55] a game for professors of literature. In the poem 'Invocación a Joyce' [Invocation to Joyce] we read: 'Fuimos el imagismo, el cubismo / los conventículos y sectas / que las crédulas universidades veneran' [We were Imagism, Cubism / the cliques and sects / that credulous universities worship].[56]

Despite Isidorre Ducasse's birth and early life in Montevideo, Borges, in 1936, dismissed him as 'intolerable'.[57] Breton in 1930 considered that the only poet worthy of attention in the past was this same Lautréamont;[58] from

---

[50] *Inquisiciones*, p. 23.

[51] *Textos cautivos*, p 328.

[52] Juan Gustavo Cobo Borda (recopilación), *El Aleph Borgiano* (Bogotá: Biblioteca Luis-Angel Arango, 1987), p 96

[53] Milan Kundera, *Testaments Betrayed An Essay in Nine Parts*, translated by Linda Asher (London. Faber, 1995), p 152

[54] *Textos cautivos*, p 64

[55] *Obra poética*, p 114.

[56] *Ibid* , p 350

[57] *Textos cautivos*, p 45.

[58] Breton, *Manifestes du Surréalisme*, p. 157.

Lautréamont came two of surrealism's founding shibboleths; the chance encounter of the sewing machine and the umbrella on the operating table, and the utopia that one day everybody would live and speak poetry (the revolutionary society of the future).

As for Rimbaud, Breton decided in 1924 that he was 'surréaliste dans la practique de la vie et ailleurs' [surrealist in the practice of life and elsewhere];[59] in 1930 Rimbaud became the most potent source for surrealist activity; his famous letter to his school teacher postulated a method for waking up the imagination, based on the 'Car JE est un autre' [For I is another][60] that grounded surrealism's exploration of the self. In 1925 Borges divided all poets into two groups; the negative ones he called 'culterano' [precious] for their love of 'la palabrera hojarasca por cariño al enmarañamiento y al relumbrón' [long-winded verbiage for love of entanglements and flashiness][61] and his first example was Rimbaud. In 1936 Borges confessed that he found Rimbaud strange and admirable for being 'aquel hombre que en posesión ilimitada de una maestría, desdeña su ejercicio y prefiere la inacción, el silencio' [that man who possesses a limitless mastery, scorns to exercise it and prefers inaction and silence],[62] but without suggesting why Rimbaud made his choice, or linking him to the great modernist temptation of silence. Borges even translated a passage from Rimbaud's *Une saison en enfer*. However, a year later Borges evoked Rimbaud as a failed visionary (in contrast to his own favourites Blake and Swedenborg): 'un artista en busca de experiencias que no logró' [an artist in quest of experiences that he could not attain].[63] In this dismissive phrase the ways part between Breton and Borges; for one, poetry was a journey into new experiences, the unknown, risk, transgression, self exploration, for the other a confirmation of an epiphanic habit.

Where Breton and Borges most obviously diverge is in their treatment of erotic love and desire. Breton's emphasis on 'l'amour charnel' [carnal love] and 'l'amour passion' [passionate love][64] led him to write: 'l'amour humain est à réédifier' [human love must be rebuilt];[65] the surrealist goal was to 'retrouver la grâce perdue du premier instant où l'on aime' [refind the grace of the first moment of falling in love];[66] all life's problems resolved in the 'folie d'un baiser' [folly of a kiss].[67] Breton: 'Il n'est pas de solution hors de l'amour' [There are no solutions outside love].[68] Borges's honesty led him to silence this

---

[59]   *Ibid.*, p 41

[60]   *Ibid*, p 250

[61]   *Inquisiciones*, pp 115-16

[62]   *Textos cautivos*, p 63

[63]   *Ibid*, p 144

[64]   Breton, *Manifestes du Surréalisme*, p 360

[65]   André Breton, *Les vases communicants* (Paris Gallimard, 1955), p 142

[66]   André Breton, *L'Amour fou* (Paris Gallimard, 1937), p. 53.

[67]   André Breton, *Point du jour* (Paris Gallimard, 1970), p 72

[68]   *Ibid*, p. 58.

emphasis, and erotic love is sadly excluded from his works.

The Parisian avant-garde, crystallising itself in the surrealist movement, forced Borges to reconsider his attitude to being a poet, and to the poem. By merging avant-garde with baroque he was able to cast aside the poet's task of interacting with 'history', and concentrate on a more perennial involvement with the muse. A factor that helped Borges define himself outside the mainstream was what Cioran called 'l'inextricable problème de la sincerité' [the inextricable problem of sincerity],[69] Lionel Trilling's 'congruence between avowal and actual feeling'.[70] The impression of sincerity poses tricky problems, but there is a tone, and an intention, that Borges, as a poet, found from his first collection *Fervor de Buenos Aires*. These poems serenely evoke the streets, sunsets and *arrabales* of Buenos Aires, the houses with their *aljibes, higueras, parras, zaguanes, patios* [cisterns, fig trees, vines, halls, patios], his 'mitología casera' [household mythology], without an ounce of irony; for Borges the poem is a space for the lyrical emotions, cocooned from the corrosion of modernity's overt irony. He wrote: 'Toda poesía es una confidencia y las premisas de cualquier confidencia son la confianza del que escucha y la veracidad del que habla' [All poetry is a confidence and the premise of all confidences is the trust of whoever listens and the truth of whoever speaks].[71] Borges once confirmed: 'escribo con sinceridad' [I write with sincerity]. He said to Cortínez that poetry was 'the only sincere thing in me'.[72]

I want now to return to Borges's poetics of timidity, the brushing aside of revolutionary change. Borges invoked the notion of insincerity when he wrote about his *ultraísta* days in 1937: 'Yo juraría, sin embargo, que predomina el agridulce sabor de la falsedad. De la insinceridad, si una palabra más cortés se requiere' [I would swear, however, that the bittersweet taste of falsity predominates. Insincerity, if a more polite word is needed].[73] He realised that the transgressive ambition of the avant-garde did not correspond to his own temperament. He could only write about what he had actually experienced – his return to Buenos Aires, his rediscovery of his roots, his forefathers, his timid loves and readings. He refused to pretend to a more prestigious literary self *a lo Rimbaud*. He categorised his self-discovery thus: 'Como los de 1969, los jóvenes de 1923 eran tímidos. Temerosos de una íntima pobreza, trataban como ahora, de escamotearla bajo inocentes novedades ruidosas' [Like those of 1969 the young of 1923 were shy. Fearful of an intimate poverty, they turned like now to hide it under innocent and noisy novelties].[74] By 'íntima pobreza' Borges meant the narrowness of life-experience. In 1926 he wrote: 'Yo he conquistado ya mi pobreza, ya he reconocido, entre miles, las nueve o diez palabras que se

---

[69] E M Cioran, *La tentation d'exister* (Paris: Gallimard, 1956), p. 179.

[70] Lionel Trilling, *Sincerity and Authenticity* (Oxford. Oxford University Press, 1972), p. 2.

[71] *El tamaño de mi esperanza*, p. 131.

[72] Cortínez, *Borges the Poet*, p 39.

[73] *Textos cautivos*, p. 97.

[74] *Obra poética*, p. 9.

llevan bien con mi corazón' [I have now conquered my poverty. Amongst thousands of words I have now recognised the nine or ten that get on well with my heart].[75] He often repeated his pride in this Franciscan poverty: 'la poesía / que es inmortal y pobre' [poetry / that is immortal and poor].[76] Sincerity forced Borges to accept this insufficiency, and make poetry out of it. Borges believed in the magic of the word ('la palabra habría sido en el principio un símbolo mágico, que la usura del tiempo gastaría. La misión del poeta sería restituir a la palabra, siquiera de un modo parcial, su primitiva y ahora oculta verdad' [In the beginning the word must have been a magical symbol that the usury of time wore out. The poet's mission would be to restore the word, even partially, to its primitive and now hidden truth]),[77] and did not dare write about experiences or desires which might cast him out of his safe lyrical space, or habits. His aesthetic timidity is based on fear: 'La raíz del lenguaje es irracional y de cáracter mágico ... La poesía quiere volver a esa antigua magia. Sin prefijadas leyes, obra de un modo vacilante y osado, como si caminara en la oscuridad' [The root of language is irrational and of a magical character. Poetry wants to return to this ancient magic. Without prearranged laws it functions in a vacilating and daring way, as if walking in the dark].[78] This quotation does not differ much from a surrealist view of the magic of language; but instead of engaging with these dark forces, Borges barely brushes them in his poetry.

Borges once selected a 1923 poem called 'Llaneza' [Plainness], dedicated to Haydée Lange (Norah Lange's sister) as his best example of 'poesía esencial'.[79] It suggests a poetics of Argentine directness, with the hint of 'llanura' and 'llano' [plain] in the title. The poem revolves around a literary gathering where everything is so familiar that 'ya están cabalmente en la memoria' [are already laid completely in memory].[80] Borges evokes how well he knows the habits and inner lives of his friends, and 'ese dialecto de alusiones / que toda agrupación humana va urdiendo' [that dialect of allusions / that all human groups contrive]; the comfort of belonging. Borges states simply: 'No necesito hablar / ni mentir privilegios; / bien me conocen quienes aquí me rodean,/ bien saben mis congojas y mi flaqueza' [I do not need to talk / to pretend privileges / those who surround me here know me well / know my anxieties and weakness]. This is heaven, to be admitted to a 'Realidad innegable, / como las piedras y los árboles' [Undeniable reality / like stones and trees]. In this cosy in-group Borges could just be himself. Cheselka saw this poem as about the security of Borges's home, not about the Lange's literary tertulia[81] at the Tronador house in Buenos Aires, but the meaning is the same.

---

[75] *El tamaño de mi esperanza*, p. 132.

[76] *Ibid* , p. 196.

[77] *La rosa profunda*, p. 10.

[78] *Obra poética*, p 115.

[79] 'Las memorias de Borges', p XI

[80] *Obras completas*, p 42

[81] Paul Cheselka, *The Poetry and Poetics of Jorge Luis Borges* (New York, Berne, Frankfurt: P Lang, 1987), pp. 77-8.

So what happened to Borges the poet between 1929 and 1960? In 'La biblioteca de Babel' [The Library of Babel] with its library of infinite, meaningless, chaotic tomes one arbitrary combination of letters leaps into a teasing fragment, a pre-Socratic snippet: 'Oh tiempo tus pirámides' [Oh time your pyramids].[82] By 1942 Borges had recreated himself as the self-reflexive ironist, the modernist whose nihilist view of the value of literature ('entreteje naderías' [it interweaves nothingnesses][83] later delighted Europe. However, the poet was still secretly there, clinging to an archaic, out-dated theory of poetry, for those words 'Oh tiempo tus pirámides' come from his own poem 'Del infierno y del cielo' [Of hell and heaven], dated 1942, as ''Oh Tiempo! tus efímeras pirámides' [Oh Time your ephemeral pyramids][84] referring to what will be obliterated by death as the poet will be confronted with a face, possibly his own, that will be heaven or hell according to how he lived his life. From this self-quotation in the library of Babel we could speculate that it's the poet in Borges, that archaic, magical *hacedor* [maker], who kept his artificial fictions alive. As Saul Yurkievich once wrote: 'Quizá el decir más esencial de Borges, aunque no el más logrado, se dé en sus poemas. Creo que Borges reserva para el verso la expersión de lo entrañable. El intento de interpretar su poesía puede revelarnos el sentido profundo de toda su obra' [Perhaps Borges's most essential sayings, although not his most worked out, can be found in his poems. I think that Borges reserves for his poetry the expression of what is most dear to him. The attempt to interpret his poetry can reveal the deep meanings of all his work].[85] Borges's self-acceptance as a poet refusing to try to bridge the gap between his timidity and the promised libertarian thrills of the avant-garde confirms César Vallejo's plea for 'honestidad espiritual'. Borges once said: 'todo lo que yo escribo es confesional' [All that I write is confessional].[86]

---

[82] *Obras completas*, p 406.

[83] Salas, *Borges Una biografía*, p. 124

[84] *Obras completas*, p. 866

[85] Saul Yurkievich, *Fundadores de la nueva poesía latinoamericana* (Barcelona: Barral Editores, 1973), p. 119.

[86] 'La última conferencia', *La Gaceta del Fondo de Cultura Económica*, No. 306, June 1996, p. 5

CHAPTER 7

Falklands/Malvinas and/as Excess:
On Simultaneous TransNation and the Poetry of War

Bernard McGuirk[*]

In the post-Falklands/Malvinas era, there has been a striking dearth of war poetry. Possibly the first poem to deal with the conflict was Jorge Luis Borges's 'Juan López y John Ward',[1] a (by no means unproblematic) translation of which appeared in *The Times* on 18 September 1982. My purpose is to situate the Borges poem in various contexts. Firstly, the Argentine writer's response to and going beyond a Wilfred Owen precursor, 'Strange Meeting', will be analysed in the light of recent poststructuralist thinking on the question of history and excess in writing. Secondly, a later Argentine poem, Susana Thénon's 'Poema con traducción simultánea Español-Español', will be contrasted with the Borges response in terms of the protocols of restraint and propriety. Thirdly, Tony Conran's 'Elegy for the Welsh Dead, in the Falkland Islands, 1982' will be considered within a Celtic 'boundary' tradition of the search for national identity beyond the glories of a patriotism-cum-jingoism. Finally, in juxtaposition with Conran's elegy, Borges's 'Milonga del muerto' will be heard as supplementing the nightmare of war with a dream of difference: precisely the *effect* on writing of history's political excesses. At respective points of the analyses, Borges's treatments of the Malvinas conflict will serve as a filter for theoretical arguments on the relationship between literature and history. The capacity of Borges and the other writers dealt with to appropriate and, at the same time, to lay bare the doubts upon which earlier traditions of war poetry often rest will be compared to the intellectual and aesthetic processes of translation. I shall argue that, though the staging of war was controlled by the Thatcher-Galtieri political manoeuvres, the theatre of its representation must continually reopen closed chapters and minds.

At the interface of literary theory and cultural studies may be traced questions both of language and of history. We have recently been reminded that 'the *question* of history is excessive with respect to history' and that 'this

---

[*] This chapter is an extended version of the 1997 *Kate Elder Memorial Lecture* delivered at Queen Mary and Westfield College of the University of London I am indebted to Maria Esther Maciel and Fabricio Forastelli for their expertise on Borges; to Alejandro Coroleu for his classical knowledge and, especially, to Tony Conran for his generosity in sending me advance extracts from his forthcoming autobiography, *Visions and Praying Mantids*. In a letter sent to me on 12 November 1997, he writes: 'I'm quite excited at the idea of people reading me in Argentina My grandfather was an engineer there and my father was born, I think in Mendoza. So it really is the land of my Fathers! It's difficult to know whether that has anything to do with the poem, but probably it gave an added feeling to the mix'
[1] Jorge Luis Borges, 'Juan Lopez and John Ward', *The Times*, London, 18 September, 1982. Also in *Los conjurados Obras completas* (Buenos Aires Emecé, 1989), vol 2, p 500

worrying excess no doubt accounts for the repeated calls 'to get back to history' and for the accusation that history is precisely what poststructuralism *lacks*.[2] Addressing that interface, and extrapolating, I shall ask whether, too, the *question* of language is (always) excessive with respect to language. In the process, questions of poetry, of translation, of politics, and of cultural difference will also be posed. And the context will be my own concern to show how 'literature highlights the differences that cultural studies explore'.[3]

As vehicle, I shall use, principally, four poems of the 1980s and 1990s. All are responses to the Malvinas/Falklands conflict; each indulges the game of the name; all might be read as disrupting too-easy assumptions regarding the representation of North-South, East-West relations; each heralds the death of the compass points of post-colonialism as expressed by always already clichéd markers of Empire and of its histories. Each resists the ready availability of *us* and *them* transcriptions – no less overtly than did the BBC refuse Margaret Thatcher's imperative, at the height of the 1982 crisis, that newscasters should cease to indulge any illusion of objectivity by substituting 'our' and 'the enemy' for 'the British' and 'the Argentine' forces. Pre-amble is also and unapologetically pre-text, an excess to be heeded prior to the opening shots, the engagements which the Borges, Thénon and Conran poems make with history. Though, as I shall argue, such poems impose delay, their delaying tactic need not be worrying... *if* we accept that literature's translation of histories and of cultures into instant recognitions, common or shared perceptions, cannot be (made) easily available. For the suffix to any *trans* will be both *late* and *gressive*... only ever performable amidst the cuts, and bearing the displaced accents of a post-poststructuralist as well as of a supposedly post-colonialist critical era.[4]

Whereas effects of language may be apprehended through its syncopes, the effectiveness of historical conflicts is usually, and suddenly, comprehended only by the strong becoming weak... or vice versa.

Juan López y John Ward

Les tocó en suerte una época extraña
El planeta había sido parcelado en distintos países, cada uno provisto
de lealtades, de queridas memorias, de un pasado sin duda heroico, de

---

[2]   Derek Attridge, Geoffrey Bennington, and Robert Young (eds.), *Post-Structuralism and the Question of History* (Cambridge: Cambridge University Press, 1988), pp. 8-9.

[3]   Bernard McGuirk, *Latin American Literature Symptoms, Risks and Strategies of Post-structuralist Criticism* (London: Routledge, 1997), p. 19.

[4]   See Michel Foucault, 'Nietzsche, Genealogy, History', *The Foucault Reader*, edited by Paul Rabinow (New York· Pantheon, 1984), p. 88. 'The traditional devices of constructing a comprehensive view of history and for retrieving the past as a patient and continuous development must be systematically dismantled Necessarily, we must dismiss those tendencies that encourage the consoling play of recognition . History becomes 'effective' to the degree that it introduces discontinuity into our very being '

derechos, de agravios, de una mitología peculiar, de
próceres de bronce, de aniversarios, de
demagogos y de símbolos. Esa división, cara a los
cartógrafos, auspiciaba las guerras.

López había nacido en la ciudad junto al río inmóvil.
Ward, en las
afueras de la ciudad por la que caminó Father Brown.
Había estudiado
castellano para leer el Quijote.
El otro profesaba el amor de Conrad, que le había sido
revelado en un
aula de la calle Viamonte.
Hubieran sido amigos, pero se vieron una sola vez cara a
cara, en unas
islas demasiado famosas, y cada uno de los dos fue Caín,
y cada uno, Abel.
Los enterraron juntos. La nieve y la corrupción los
conocen.
El hecho que refiero pasó en un tiempo que no podemos
entender.

Jorge Luis Borges, Clarín, 1982

Juan López and John Ward

It was their fate to live in a strange time.
The planet had been carved into different countries,
each one provided with loyalties, with loved memories,
with a past which doubtless had been heroic, with
ancient and recent traditions, with rights, with grievances,
with its own mythology, with
forebears in bronze, with anniversaries, with demagogues
and
with symbols. Such an arbitrary division was favourable
to war.

López had been born in the city next to the motionless
river; Ward in the outskirts of the city
through which
Father Brown had walked. He had studied Spanish
so as to read the *Quixote*.
The other professed a love of Conrad, revealed
to him in a class in Viamonte Street.
They might have been friends, but they saw each other
just once,
face to face, in islands only too well known, and each one

was Cain and each
one, Abel.

They buried them together. Snow and corruption
know them.

The story I tell happened in a time we cannot
understand.

Jorge Luis Borges, *The Times*, 1982
translated by Rodolfo Terragno

So be it? Amen? The construction of an opening gambit of Olympian
distance, impersonality, objectivity, disinterest, a refusal to take sides, a mere
'naming of parts' ... thus might the word 'fate' be seen to operate, reiterating a
classical trope of juxtaposing destiny with the 'strangeness' of time, as if history
were always in excess not only of its writing but also of our understanding of it.
The apparent predetermination implicit in the division of the planet into
potentially martial factions would make it appear that, not for the first time, here
is a Borges going transcendental; opting for the difference between countries as
predestined, unavoidable point of departure on a road to cyclically repeated
wars. According to the terms of such an irresistible polarity, the only predictable
construct would be that of Nationalisms, Histories writ large, official versions,
'lealtades' to be tested, and attested, by check-lists of 'pasado', 'heroico',
'queridas memorias', 'aniversarios'. The writing-implements of such a polarised
reading of history are meticulously mapped: 'derechos' and 'agravios'. Thereby
a mythology has been produced and, in Borges's representation of it, is shown to
be inseparable from proprietary rights and ownership. The reality effects of such
strong myths are the hammered bronze echoes of anniversaries, the resonance of
demagoguery and the unequivocality of symbols. Only once in the opening
sequence of the poem has a 'sin duda' crept in, near-casual prefiguration – its
ironising frame easily missable – of an overt, a sententious, and, thus far, it
might seem, a dangerously unopposed, omniscient voicing: 'Esa división ...
auspiciaba las guerras' [less meticulously mapped – without, indeed, any
cartographers at all – in Terragno's 'Such an arbitrary division was favourable to
war'].

Before addressing the private pasts and the public uniformities of the two
J****s, I venture to admit that, were any old-fashioned structuralists still about,
they would ('sin duda') detect here a covert invitation to read Saussurean lessons
into this late-Borges treatment of history.[5] As in the case of all closed meanings,
the planet-wide carve-up into differing Nationalisms, into different signifieds,

---

[5]   For example: 'Just as Saussure demonstrated that there was no relationship between the sign
and the idea other than the agreed but arbitrary, Borges's text effectively disabuses the reader of
any expectation of an agreed solution (a signified) deriving from a familiar generic formal pattern
(a signifier)'. McGuirk, *Latin American Literature*, p 128

might indeed have been for too long read as ordained by fate and agreed by men ... agreed but arbitrary, and with no positive terms. Read retrospectively, however, the 'distintos países' of the opening sequence might be said to require a re-writing of their respective histories in excess of the confining term(inology), the straitjacket of those nationalising ideologies which endow countries with auguries, auspicious or ill, both of, and for, war. It is in this light, therefore, that the word 'auspiciaba' might be said to point to an over-dominant metaphysics, the supposedly unavoidable (and historically repeated) resolution of conflicting mythologies of nation through military confrontation.

As the Juan López and John Ward of Borges's text are schooled in the respective *loci* of their differential fates, the private and public strands of their lives (their perusal of Conrad or Cervantes, their perambulations along the River Plate or through Chesterton's suburbs) are interwoven only to lead them to the particularity of their signifying encounter.[6] This particularity is not just constructed on difference but, I shall now argue, on *différence*, too. The specificity of the brief attributions to Buenos Aires and London is complemented by a prolonged disclosure of, and an openness to, reciprocity and its potential. An encountering without othering is tentatively approached via Juan and John as *literati*, through their readerly preparing for, their conceiving of, the translatability of a *mediated* other – that Other filtered through literatures, through traditions, through societies, and which consists of cultural difference. The hypothetical status of such *un*reality effects is however confined, consigned, to but a short sentence, 'Hubieran sido amigos', before the onset, the onrush, of a more divisive outcome ... the interbayonetry of that form of cultural transfer which will always set its face against negotiated settlement (of differences).

In an 'una sola vez', in sheer instantaneity, does the Borges text confront the meeting of faces (though not of eyes). In the borrowed terms of narrative analysis, the only available sphere of action is the double actant space where each is Cain and each is Abel. For the absolute narrative, transcendent History, can cope with, will apportion, no blame, no fault, no right, no wrong. In such an ironised story, the Juan/John 'suerte' is, inevitably, both to live and to die in 'una época extraña'... buried together under the cover not of darkness but of a more pervasive, chilling, snowy blankness ... and the corruption of a shared, a *same* death, which, macabre aspiration, abolishes the difference of self and other, self in other. A *same* death which permits no story, no history of their difference, their common particularity, resolved or dissolved in the illusory coming together of the time and its telling. But is 'un tiempo que no podemos entender' merely a conclusive note of resignation to fate, to strangeness, to incomprehensibility? Or an invitation to read *back* through the poem, attempting to listen not to what *'we'* cannot understand but rather to the fact *'I'* tell? The excessive relation of the individual's voicing to simultaneous histories-become-History constitutes an invitation to listen again, whether to the Borges poem or

---

[6]   See my discussion of Francisco Delich's juxtaposition of the *particular* with the Hegelian public versus private (*ibid*, pp 12-13)

to the official spokesmen of the Thatcher Government, the Ian Macdonalds, the John Notts ... What we are asked to hear is a counterpoint to the clipped, flat, matter-of-fact intoning cultivatedly understating the course, and the discourse, of a history of the excessively famous, the notorious. Thus the Borges poem subverts, even as it broaches, the construction of dangerous clichés of *in*difference; will not allow Juan and John an infamous loss of particular identities whereby they are turned into 'The Unknown Soldier', become transfused by, confused with, a sentimentalising *dulce et decorum est pro patria mori* ... Particular differences *between* Juan and John should be no less legible now than is that instance of *différence* at play *within* Juan López and John Ward; the projected inscription of Jorge Luis's own initials into a relationship with the (linguistic?) Other overtly inscribed by both trace and excess of *intra*textual conflicts.

Counterpoint and excess also serve to characterise the relation of the Borges poem to its Wilfred Owen precursor:[7]

Strange Meeting
It seemed that out of battle I escaped
Down some profound dull tunnel, long since scooped
Through granites which titanic wars had groined.
Yet also there encumbered sleepers groaned,
Too fast in thought or death to be bestirred.
Then, as I probed them, one sprang up, and stared
With piteous recognition in fixed eyes,
Lifting distressful hands as if to bless.
And by his smile, I knew that sullen hall,
By his dead smile I knew we stood in Hell.
With a thousand pains that vision's face was grained;
Yet no blood reached there from the upper ground,
And no guns thumped, or down the flues made moan.
'Strange friend,' I said, 'here is no cause to mourn.'
'None,' said that other, 'save the undone years,
The hopelessness. Whatever hope is yours,
Was my life also; I went hunting wild
After the wildest beauty in the world,
Which lies not calm in eyes, or braided hair,
But mocks the steady running of the hour,
And if it grieves, grieves richlier than here.
For of my glee might many men have laughed,
And of my weeping something had been left,
Which must die now. I mean the truth untold,
The pity of war, the pity war distilled.
Now men will go content with what we spoiled,

---

[7]   Wilfred Owen, in Jon Silkin (ed), *The Penguin Book of First World War Poetry* (Harmondsworth: Penguin Books, 1982), pp. 196-8.

Or, discontent, boil bloody, and be spilled.
They will be swift with swiftness of the tigress.
None will break ranks, though nations trek from progress.
Courage was mine, and I had mystery,
Wisdom was mine and I had mastery:
To miss the march of this retreating world
Into vain citadels that are not walled.
Then, when much blood had clogged their chariot-wheels,
I would go up and wash them from sweet wells,
Even with truths that lie too deep for taint.
I would have poured my spirit without stint
But not through wounds; not on the cess of war.
Foreheads of men have bled where no wounds were.
I am the enemy you killed, my friend.
I knew you in this dark: for so you frowned
Yesterday through me as you jabbed and killed.
I parried; but my hands were loath and cold.
Let us sleep now...'

Wilfred Owen

Direct echoes are muted but an overt interpellation in Borges's opening line, 'extraña', convokes both title and the ghosts from Owen's face-to-face encounter in Hell in order to pre-figure his own protagonists' entrenched inseparability in an all-too-similar 'profound dull tunnel'. Owen's first-person – 'out of battle escaped' only to confront his also dead adversary of but yesterday's jab and parry – is allowed a point of view:

'Strange friend', I said, 'here is no cause to mourn.'
'None', said that other, 'save the undone years,
The hopelessness. Whatever hope is yours,
Was my life also [...]'

Borges, however, ethically refraining, one might argue, from any identifying relation with the combatant-Owen's option for eerie dramatic dialogue, borrows only the hypothetical. 'Hubieran sido amigos' performs the defamiliarisation necessary to his own respectful visit to the grave of the predecessor's poem ... and his strategic retreat from it. If Borges's Juan and John are not permitted to enter such an exchange as 'I am the enemy you killed, my friend. I know you in this dark', it is because of an *excess*. In appropriating but requiring to go beyond Wilfred Owen's 'Strange Meeting', the later poem reminds us too that it is written after the era of *La Grande Illusion*: 'pero se vieron una sola vez cara a cara'. Concomitantly, Owen's 'Let us sleep now...' finds in Borges's 'Los enterraron juntos' a counterpart but without hint of consolation. 'My hands were loath and cold' derives from a personal voice not available in the Argentine's bleaker rendering of the icy effect of war: 'La nieve y la corrupción los conocen'. Thus is the final line of the Borges poem prepared for: facts? history?

Such events as have rendered *too* famous mere outcrops of the south Atlantic must exceed understanding; confound nationalistic apportionings of roles of right and wrong; allow for no making capital out of *H*istory; refuse the writing of *M*yth.

The Falklands Conflict, as it was called, came, however, to represent – to a British public many of whom did not even know where the islands lay at the time of the first, South Georgia, 'invasion' by the Argentine troops – a particularly dominant metaphysics of presence in the strife-torn early 1980s phase of the Margaret Thatcher years. Amongst the scandalously repressed absences of that period of burning UK inner-cities, of strikes and counter strikes – Brit *versus* grit – was the term *Malvinas,* itself repressing another by now faint imperial echo, less of Britain's 'naming of parts' than of Britanny's parting with names – St Malo, whence *Les Iles Maloines.* Now, out of France, in a late twentieth-century rivalry of post-imperial but never post-economic colonising powers, was cast the shadow not of Breton exiles ... but of bolt-on Exocets. The creation of a meta-geography (and a metal market) favourable to war suggests that the ever bullish economy of Nationalism emerged, in April 1982, as a fragmentary narrative of half-locatable places where, with stunning rapidity, all-too-situable visages (of power) *chose* to come face-to-face. Perhaps not apocryphally, the Galtieri-Thatcher struggle over southern (dis)comfort on the rocks is said to have been described by Jorge Luis Borges as that of 'two bald men fighting over a comb'.

North
⇕
South

My re-reading of political, no less than of literary, representations – always in excess of themselves – is a translation, or a betrayal, inspired in me by a second cultural and linguistic interface (or cutting), one addressed head-on, in a poem from her 1987 collection *Ova completa*, by the Argentine writer Susana Thénon:[8]

Poema con traducción simultánea Español-Español

> *Para ir hacia lo venidero*
> *para hacer, si no el paraíso,*
> *la casa feliz del obrero*
> *en la plenitud ciudadana,*
> *vínculo íntimo eslabona*
> *e ímpetu exterior hermana*

---

[8]   Susana Thénon, *Ova completa* (Buenos Aires· Editorial Sudamericana, 1987), pp. 27-8.

a la raza anglosajona
con la latinoamericana.

Rubén Darío. *Canto a la Argentina*

Cristóforo
  (el Portador de Cristo)
hijo de un humilde cardador de lana
  (hijo de uno que iba por lana sin cardar)
zarpó del puerto de Palos
  (palo en zarpa dejó el puerto)
no sin antes persuadir a Su Majestad la Reina
Isabel la Católica de las bondades de la empresa
por él concebida
  (no sin antes persuadir a Her Royal Highness
  die Königin Chabela la Logística de empeñar
  la corona en el figón de Blumenthal con-verso)
así se vertiesen litros y litros de
genuina sangre vieja factor RH negativo
  (así costase sangre sudor y lágrimas
  antípodas)

se hicieron a la mar
  (se hicieron alamares)
y tras meses y meses de yantar solo
oxímoron en busca de la esquiva redondez
  (y tras días y días de mascar Yorkshire pudding
  y un pingüino de añadidura los domingos)
alguno exclamó tierra
  (ninguno exclamó thálassa)

desembarcaron
en 1492 a.D.
  (pisaron
  en 1982 a.D.)
jefes esperaban
en pelota
genuflexos
  (mandamases aguardaban
  desnudos
  de rodillas)
Cristóforo gatilló el misal
  (Christopher disparó el misil)
dijo a sus pares
  (murmuró a sus secuaces)
coño

(fuck)
ved aquí nuevos mundos
  (ved aquí estos inmundos)
quedáoslos
  (saqueadlos)
por Dios y Nuestra Reina
  (por Dios y Nuestra Reina)

AMÉN

(OMEN)

Susana Thénon

Poem with Simultaneous Translation Spanish to Spanish

To move towards what is still to come,
to construct, if not paradise,
the happy house of the worker
in the plenitude of the city,
intimate bond ties
and outer strength unites in brotherhood
the Anglosaxon race
with the Latin American.

Rubén Darío, *Song to the Argentine*

Cristóforo
  (the Bearer of Christ)
son of a humble carder of wool
  (son of one who went for wool without carding)
cast anchor from the port of Palos
  (stick in his grasp he left the port)
not without first persuading Her Majesty the Queen
Isabel the Catholic of the goodnesses of the enterprise
by him conceived
  (not without first persuading Her Royal Highness
  die Königin Chabela of the Logistics of pawning
  the crown in the eating-house of Blumenthal con-vert)
so as to spill litres and litres of
genuine old blood factor RH negative
  (so as to cost blood sweat and tears
  antipodean)

they made out to sea
  (they made decorative fastenings)
and after months and months of vitt'ling alone
oxymoron in search of the elusive roundness
  (and after days and days of chewing on Yorkshire pudding
  and a penguin in addition on Sundays)
one of them cried land
  (none of them cried thálassa)

they disembarked
in 1492 AD
  (they trod
  in 1982 AD)
chiefs were waiting
stark naked
genuflecting
  (bosses waited
  stripped
  kneeling)
Cristóforo triggered the missal
  (Christopher fired the missile)
said to his peers
  (whispered to his followers)
coño
  (fuck)
see here new worlds
  (see here these unwashed)
keep them
  (sack them)
for God and our Queen
  (for God and our Queen)

AMEN

(OMEN)

Susana Thénon (my translation)

If the somewhat less than celebratory pre-quincentenary gift of Prime Minister Thatcher to the Galtieri regime came ten years too early, at least the unseemly rush across the South Atlantic, again to see and sack new worlds, allowed Thénon the time (she died in 1990) to situate the *translatability* of inseparably monarchic, ecclesiastical and military post-colonialism as not only a clichéd North-South, English-Spanish, relation but also as an effect shown to be operative between Spanish and Spanish, between Spanish American and Spanish Americans. Here, Thénon shows up the virtual taboo-subject of *intra-*

colonialism. Within the political/ideological frontiers of Spanish America, there would appear to be a need *not* (only) for translation of the message of resistance against cyclical colonising aggression into the language (English) of its latest perpetrators but (also) for its repetition, in difference, to the often indifferent (Spanish American) other.

The very title of Thénon's poem broaches (humorously?) the problematic issue of difference *within* as opposed to the more conventional difference *between* languages. However many millions the United Nations might spend on the provision of simultaneous translation, its peacemaking services will always founder amidst the kind of pious idealism or melting pot Utopianism encapsulated by, but not restricted to, the Rubén Darío epigraph. Seldom will a rhyme be so ironised as when *eslabona/anglosajona*, read retrospectively and *after* Thénon's text, rattle out, in (un)chained melodrama, the bond(age) of brotherhood links. Here, the South-to-North 'vínculo' metaphor is no less prone to a solution-cum-pollution, cure-cum-poison reading than is Jacques Derrida's *pharmakon*. For Thénon's poem undoes many a familiar metaphysics. Not least a time-honoured adoptive practice whereby Darío is appropriated as honorary Argentine; whereby over-awareness of cultural difference struggles with under-bewareness of dependency; whereby a high-serious tradition of Buenos Aires *literati* resistance to the condescendingly deemed 'facile' word-play of such as *Ova completa* is contestatorily pastiched by Thénon's intervention. The sacrosanct territory of Jorge Luis Borges's meditation on *non*-simultaneous Spanish-to-Spanish translation, in 'Pierre Menard, Autor del Quijote', is revisited. Here, in what effectively operates as 'Margaret Thatcher, Author of The Conquest', the precursor Columbus cannot be (agonically) engaged with ... without excess. An excess of history and an excess of language. The official version will ever be shadowed by the parenthetic (trace of) supplementarity.

A clichéd *traduttore/TRADITORE* view of translation need not be confined to language; the question of history as repetition, as action replay, is posed only to be deposed; 'source' [language] is mined only to be undermined; 'target' [language] will be gauged by missal *and* missile ... intertextuality *qua* infra-red brutality. Playing the translation game, Thénon's poem indulges an illusory binary of past versus present, 1492 versus 1982, (West-seeking) aetiology versus (heat-seeking) teleology. It is as if the brackets which represent, visually, the simultaneous translator's version were, auditively, ear-phones conveying the message of a constant, and sardonic, interference.

'Cristóforo', linguistically and culturally foreign to the Spanish ear – Genoese commoner in spite of the Greek grandeur of his name's etymology – might be retrospectively *interpreted* as the Bearer of Christ to the New World though, to the pretentious contemporaries of the court of the *Reyes Católicos*, he was but the importunately supplicant son of a wool-weaver ... only much later to be Agnus-deified. (Crackling through the ear-phones come the interfering obscenities: on the make via 'lana'/lucre; but not scoring via 'sin cardar'/without *screwing*?) The historic casting of the anchor of Discovery from the Southern

Spanish port of Palos de Moguer echoes excessively (clenched in the fist is the sword-cross staff of the Conquistador). Lest we forget Enterprise Culture, the bonds no less of 1492 than of 1982, and should the near-equivalent Isabeline/Elizabethan(II) coincidences not suffice, the Christ-bearer *impressario* must serve Her Catholic Majesty with both goodness and *bounty* ... never forgetting a courtier's syntax. (The *logos* of persuasion in the Windsor-once-Saxe-Coburg Gothic transference is multiply scrambled. HRH the Princess Lilibet is infantilised, in echo of the Infanta Chabela [=diminutive of Isabel], persuaded to pledge the seal of Royal Appointment, the Crown-pawned conversion of HM fleet at the dictat of the all-consuming military Logistics of the Falklands War Effort. A monetarist's bargain struck over a cheap me(t)al in a 'figón'? By smooth tonguing [con-verso/with-verse]? Conversely, background noise might be un-jammed ... Blumenthal, persecuted, exterminated by fifteenth-century Spaniards and twentieth-century Germans (or Argentines) alike, but never wholly expellable, or silenced. Is *con-verso* the Jew trans-ported, rather than integrally converted? ... and, by the way, was Colombus himself a New Christian?) The propaganda line(age) of *limpieza de sangre* – genuine dynasty or not – intermingles RHesus/Royal Highness with the negative factor guaranteed to spill New World blood (or, in a Churchillian rhetoric revamped for the Task Force of Albion's Expedition to the South Atlantic, the 'blood, sweat and tears' of an Antipodean adventurism. Shall 'we' *always* fight them on the beaches ... whatever the cost?).

And so to sea (and sew to see the officers' braid? Press-studded by the press-ganged?). Old time-spans of months on board and the archaism 'yantar' recall the first voyage of Colombus, months of unrelenting flat(Earth)ness with nothing to ingest but solitude and air. The proximity of oxymoron to oxygen – in echo of the expression 'comer aire'? – encapsulates the sharp-dull ache of the epic (but, for the near mutinous hungry sailors, the unrelenting) failure to reach the Indies by sailing West. (For the 'Brits', nearly five centuries on, the speedier expeditionary rhythm cannot disguise the chewing monotony. For them, separation from home means no (trace of) roast beef with the Yorkshire pudding, let alone the (difference of) beefing about Mrs Thatcher's 'enemy within', the Yorkshire miners – only *The Sun*-style (supplement of) penguin-stereotyping ... *10 Things You Didn't Know About The 'Argies'*?)

The operation of 'worrying' linguistic excess, up to this point in Thénon's poem, has made any repeat-call 'to get back to history' but a reminder that the *discourse* of history, too, comes laden with between-the-lines reading possibilities not that poststructuralism *lacks* but, I shall argue, that deconstructive strategies must elicit. For the textualising of the climactic event of the *annus mirabilis* is framed thus:

> one of them cried land
> (none of them cried thálassa)

What access can there be to tone, other than through the supplementarity of a saturated translation? The dry relief of arrival at the *terra incognita* of the Other finds expression (always) against the intertext of linguistic difference and, here, of historico-literary *différance*. Before the encounter with, fear of, the Other can turn into xenophobia, Xenophon-through-ear-phone intrudes in a (quasi-) simultaneous translation. *Thálassa!* – cry of blissful return homewards, from Mesopotamia to 'civilisation' of war-weary Greeks – is the crafty classicist Susana Thénon's own oxymoronic landfall-seaview reminiscence of *Anabasis* (401 BC) – inverted prefiguration of the poem's doubled 'a.D.' basis. Written dates now perform in *excessive* relation one to the other, highlighting the limitations of the frame of history. *Un*repeatability, *un*translatability allow *particular* perceptions of political events to resist such blanket rallying calls to imperial adventurism as that of a Churchill-echoing Iron Lady of 1982. The 'a.D.' repetition has acquired, via the covert classical BC precursor text, not only a historical comparison but also, with renewed emphasis, a religious difference. An Athenian nationalism under reconstruction was the backcloth to the expedition of Xenophon, 'one of the "Ten Thousand" Greeks who went to Asia to seek their fortune, unaware till it was too late to withdraw that Cyrus meant to win the Persian empire by a blow directed deep into its heart'.[9] Any 'unawareness' on the part of the *conquistadores* is no less open to interrogation as 'disembarked' becomes 'trod'. Four hundred and ninety years on, the effect of historical accuracy and objectivity in the representation of Discovery is undermined by the echoing tread of Christendom's inseparably colonising-proselytising mission. For lurking in the background is 'la Católica'/'la Logística', the Church Militant, ever crushing underfoot the serpent of an eternally sinful Edenic barbarism. Thénon's poem also feeds on oxymoron.

The archetypal primal scene of North-South/East-West encounter is re-enacted in rapid-fire rhythms as the tread-mark of post-Freudian as well as of post-colonial imprinting is trans-scribed. Cristopher Colombus, Bernal Díaz de Castilla, Pero Vaz da Caminha, scriptors all, shadow the official résumé: hierarchy in suspense, raw nakedness, religious submission (belatedly: Argentine 'guv'nors' on tenterhooks, stripped, on their knees). And the phantom-scribes in the translation from Santo Domingo to Port Stanley? 'Our' own correspondents. Un-author-ised versions. There are moments when critical theory is too facilely abused. Roland Barthes's 'Death of The Author', polemically targeted to shift authority from source to readership, has too often been (mis)read as loading language alone with responsibility for mediations. Yet it is, above all, *cultural* translation that threatens the cosiness expressed in his rhetorical 'writing is that neutral, composite, oblique space where our subject slips away, the negative where all identity is lost'.[10] An excess of language, in relation not only to its *self* but also to its *other*, is exposed by a poem constructed on that very equivalence deconstructed by its own performative translation. An excess of history, too, is revealed in the surplus moral (re-)armament of the missal (missile). Christ is borne on the trace(r)-bullet-points of binary bearers,

[9]   *Encyclopaedia Britannica* (London, 1963), vol 23, p. 836.
[10]   Roland Barthes, 'The Death of the Author', *Image Music Text* (London: Fontana, 1982), p. 142

preached (hissed) to peers (or followers) ... apostles all. And who are these disciples to punish? The expletive, somewhat unusually in the documenting of history, remains *un*deleted in official and unofficial versions. Translation intervenes only as an intensifier. Force, contempt, sex, obscenity... transgression. Behold new worlds/Go forth and multiply *possession*. (Behold these unwashed 'Argies'/*Gotcha*!)

The intonation would appear to be univocal as the text approaches its Vespers. For the only time, the ear-phone parentheses apparently contain the self-same locution in the translation as in the original: 'por Dios y Nuestra Reina' (bis). Faithful? Where linguistic and historical difference disappear is in *cliché*, language emptied of particularity, the imprecation which carries us once more onto the breach of all nations at war. Fateful? Or avoidable as soon as differential reading is allowed? For the boomed imperative of faith-*full* resignation AMÉN faces faith-*less* future when translated with the *inclusion* of a supplementarity borrowed, perhaps, from the opening line of the epigraph: 'para ir hacia lo venidero'. If the *question* of history, if the *question* of language, if all *questions* of representation are, indeed, always already excessive with respect to histories, languages and representations, then the 'So be it' of Church and State conformity will always be the least digestible of imperatives. The slippage from AMÉN to (OMEN) supplements South-to-North vassalage with a warning of resistance to all unquestioned assumptions regarding translation and translatability. In the politicisation of deconstructive practices, the necessary supplementarities, in any case, are to be traced not only between the lines and between the cultures, but also *within*. My early claim that Susana Thénon's poem confronts *intra*-colonialism inseparably from its uncompounded progenitor needs be re-addressed now only by re-posing the *question* of the repeatability of AMÉN within *Latin America*. So be it?

To any and every Latin American who has said, since 1982, 'What *we* need is a Margaret Thatcher', the poem pleads 'coño' (and only in brackets '(fuck)' for the Anglo-Saxons who never listen until it suits them). For in the wings, always opportunist, are the listeners – on the inside as well as on the outside – who will (mis)interpret the plea, hear differently the same words. For those Latin Americans who still regard their own history and language as subordinate to their *empresa* – ¿Cristóforos? – prayer will easily be (mis)read as imprecation, invitation ... '(ved aquí estos inmundos)' ... '(saqueadlos)' ... '(OMEN)'. From *within*, too, comes the subversion, the ominous call for outside intervention by those who have always (ever ready) been poised to pounce, and to sack – '(fuck)'.

West ⇔ East

A discredited counterpoint of West-East effects will now have already been represented by scenes chosen from that England conceived of as 'back home' in the roast-beef-and-Yorkshire-pudding imaginary of the 1982 Task Force. For the wounded deprived of a place in the front ranks of triumphalism at the London Falklands Victory Parade, being hidden away as the 'negative factor' surplus to representation of the Nation, here was, perhaps, an unintended opportunity. A chance to ponder their exclusion from the (national) front-row as being strangely in keeping with the relegated role of millions of other Britons? One function of this *coda* might be to reflect again, if not always, on the internal differences at work *within* the 'United' Kingdom just before and, after, intensified, the so-called external (translated?) Malvinas conflict was over. For those in Britain who ask why so little poetry of war has derived from the Falklands-Malvinas conflict, the present meditation can provide only indirect answer. A televisual age – as in the case of Vietnam, The Gulf, Bosnia – has spawned its literary responses in such dramas as *Tumbledown.* When we find a counterpart in English to both the texts of the Argentine poets and to literary representations of the plight of 'los chicos de la guerra', the voice comes from a site and from a history of very particular enunciation. 'Back home' is neither England nor at one with, or even in, a united realm:

Elegy for the Welsh Dead, in the Falkland Islands, 1982

> *Gwyr a aeth Gatraeth oedd ffraeth eu ilu.*
> *Glasfedd eu hancwyn, a gwenwyn fu.*

> B Y Gododdin (6th century)

(Men went to Catraeth, keen was their company.
They were fed on fresh mead, and it proved poison.)

Men went to Catraeth. The luxury liner
For three weeks feasted them.
They remembered easy ovations,
Our boys, splendid in courage.
For three weeks the albatross roads,
Passwords of dolphin and petrel,
Practised their obedience
Where the killer whales gathered,
Where the monotonous seas yelped.
Though they went to church with their standards
Raw death has them garnished.

Men went to Catraeth. The Malvinas
Of their destiny greeted them strangely,
Instead of affection there was coldness,
Splintering iron and the icy sea,
Mud and the wind's malevolent satire.
They stood nonplussed in the bomb's indictment.
Malcolm Wigley of Connah's Quay. Did his helm
Ride high in the war-line?

Did he drink enough mead for that journey?
The desolated shores of Tegeingl,
Did they pig this steel that destroyed him?
The Dee runs silent beside empty foundries.
The way of the wind and the rain is adamant.

Clifford Elley of Pontypridd. Doubtless he feasted.
He went to Catraeth with a bold heart.
He was used to valleys. The shadow held him.
The staff and the fasces of tribunes betrayed him.
With the oil of our virtue we have anointed
His head, in the presence of foes.

Phillip Sweet of Cwmback. Was he shy before girls?
He exposes himself now to the hags, the glance
Of the loose-fleshed whores, the deaths
That congregate like gulls on garbage.
His sword flashed in the wastes of nightmare.

Russell Carlisle of Rhuthun. Men of the North
Mourn Rhegd's son in the castellated vale.
His nodding charger neighed for the battle.
Uplifted hooves pawed at the lightning.
Now he lies down. Under the air he is dead.

Men went to Catraeth. Of the forty-three
Certainly Tony Jones of Carmarthen was brave.
What did it matter, steel in the heart?
Shrapnel is faithful now. His shroud is frost.

With the dawn men went. Those forty-three,
Gentlemen all, from the streets and byways of Wales,
Dragons of Aberdare, Denbigh and Neath –
Figment of empire, whore's honour, held them.
Forty-three at Catraeth died for our dregs.

Tony Conran[11]

Tony Conran's exploiting of the ironies of the sixth-century epigraph from an epic precedent is both more harshly focused and structurally elaborated than was Thénon's scathing mockery of Rubén Darío's ingenuous panamericanism. The threads of difference *within*, on the British side, are unwoven and re-knitted in a grim tapestry of wars separated less by kind than by the centuries and by vernaculars. If there is any, however rickety, unifying frame, it can only derive

---

[11]   Tony Conran, in Dannie Abse (ed), *Twentieth Century Anglo-Welsh Poetry* (Bridgend· Seren, Poetry Wales Press, 1997), pp 155-6

from a Welshness in-the-making ... and, plaintively, in simultaneous destruction. For what keeps on coming, and coming, is that cyclical move from valley and mountain and quayside and cawl; to poisoned mead and to Catraeth – or, in this case, Bluff Cove – as carrion. The modern poem comes in English to its Welsh precursor of Aneirin's *Y Gododdin* much as Borges's text in Spanish revisited that of Wilfred Owen's English. Always and already at work is resistance to any hegemony of language or of history, or of dominance imposed on a cultural expression ever struggling to remind the present of its betrayed but still differential past. The poem's text does not render explicit the political dilemma of the many in Wales who, in 1982, could but show reluctance to enter military conflict against an Argentina which, still, and famously, harboured the Welsh settlements, and Welsh-speaking communities, of Patagonia. Where were to be heard – in Whitehall not so loudly, now, it seemed – the historic arguments on kith and kin which, as recently as Rhodesian UDI of 1965, had advocated jaw-jaw not war-war? Memories of the Harold Wilson–Ian Smith dialogues of HMS *Tiger* ... (now, again, 'el otro tigre', alas) had but recently been burning bright, and well into the Knight, in the glowing reputation of that same Lord Peter Carrington who, since gun-boat was here to triumph over diplomacy, resigned, leaving the stage of, and to, Margaret Thatcher's monologic, steps-of-Downing Street, imperative: 'Rejoice! Rejoice!'. Conran's poem, in turn, must find its counterpoint and, again, must perform in a relation of excess.

The carding and weaving I shall carry out on the Thénon and Conran texts, and the dye of Borges and of Owen with which they are tinted, are but coincidental, never accidental effects. In his archiving of First World War poetry's resources, Jon Silkin catalogues patriotic cant; angry prophecy; compassion; desire for change.[12] Parallels beckon. Notes of triumphalism, celebration, feasting. Whether the reference to the incited euphoria of war preparations be sixth-century Welsh, fifteenth-century Spanish, or early *and* late twentieth-century British, it is the 'easy ovations' that are most facilely remembered. The Conran and Thénon poems, it is obvious, opt for the interpersonal. Conran's juxtaposition of 'luxury' and 'feast' with the chill reality of a South Atlantic 'raw death' as 'garnish' is (strange meeting!) close to Thénon's discursive fauna. For her parodic 'penguins', read Conran's subversive shift from Romantic albatross routes – à L'Invitation au voyage' or 'The Rime of the Ancient Mariner' – via all-too-transparent military coding ('Passwords of dolphin and petrel') to the most realistic metaphor of the danger of the South Atlantic for the obedient men who, again, went to Catraeth: the near-homonym echoes starkly ... 'killer W(h)ales'. Again, as in Thénon's 'missal'/'missile' play, the formidable alliance of Church and Military both raises and sets the (ethical?) 'standards'. If one function of religion is to prepare men for it, neither garb nor garnish can ever disguise the most 'raw' of death's realities.

A recurring feature of the Owen, the Borges and now the Conran treatment of war in poetry is their keynote: 'strange'; 'extraña'; 'strangely'. The

---

[12]   Silkin, *First-World War Poetry*, pp 30-34

unavoidable sense of bewilderment encapsulated most explicitly by Borges's line 'El hecho que refiero pasó en un tiempo que no podemos entender' has been shown, already, to be but one, perhaps the simplest, mode of *ostranenie*, or literature's 'making strange'. For Thénon, dinningly repeated consecutive translations of political and cultural untranslatabilities, by juxtaposing Hispanic and Anglo-Saxon inherited imperial paradigms, made a mockery of the very notion of simultaneity, of shared perceptions, of any common humanity in such *un*strange meetings as the coming together of imperial *clichés*. The strategy of Tony Conran is almost identical to that of Jorge Luis Borges, the naming not of parts, but of names. The 'making strange', in both cases, becomes inseparable from a 'making familiar'. For Borges, emblematic Juan and John, for Conran, plural reality effects akin to the cenotaph's, the memorial's, naming of the dead, and of the home and circumstance, the place and time of each. To Silkin's catalogue might be added a perhaps too obvious resource of any poetry of war: *testimony*.

At the funeral of Pablo Neruda, in September 1973, only days after the murder of his friend and colleague the Chilean President, Salvador Allende, the people turned out – facing great danger in the guise of police brutality, military detention and torture, the 'raw' reality of instant disappearance. No less raw was the chant they voiced in dialogic unison. As some shouted out the name 'Pablo Neruda', yet others chorused 'Presente, presente'. Death not as absence but, in the rejoicing over a name, names, as a forcefully reconstituted presence. Nothing new, hardly original, but a technique that the Conran poem exploits so that the named *and* numbered Welsh dead ('forty three' of them) can never be wholly excluded from history; need not be relegated as 'excessive' to the needs of another Nation's capital victory-parade ... as was to be the lot of their surviving, wounded, or disfigured fellow combatants.

Malcolm Wigley of Connah's Quay. Present. Clifford Elley of Pontypridd. Present. Phillip Sweet of Cwmback. Present. Russell Carlisle of Ruthun. Present. Tony Jones of Carmarthen. Present... Yet it is also the past that is reconstructed by Conran's poem. For the naming function stretches back: 'Men of the North/Mourn Rhegd's son in the castellated vale' re-broaches, before the return to a refrained 'Men went to Catraeth', the historic legacy of betrayal with which the poem began. *Y Goddodin*'s epic Welsh language is borne elegiacally in echo through the place names of Tegeingl, Pontypridd, Cwmback, Ruthun, Carmarthen, Aberdare, Denbigh and Neath, until transferred to 'The Malvinas (note Conran's chosen *version* of the Islands' name) of their destiny' by 'Those forty-three/Gentlemen all' – dragons caught up in, and out, by that deadly myth, 'Figment of empire'. Borges bridled. Thénon lampooned. Conran sneers.

The excessive relationship of myth to history can be seen to operate in a further, perhaps more complex process of naming. The Conran poem does not leap from the 6th to the 20th century in an indifferentiated scream of patriotism. National difference and cultural identities are explored in complex social layers whereby the politics that spawned the Falklands War effort are deemed to be inseparable from the names of men and of communities so fatally affected:

> The desolated shores of Tegeingl,
> Did they pig this steel that destroyed him?
> The Dee runs silent beside empty foundries.
> The way of the wind and the rain is adamant.

As adamant as Maggie and 'not for turning'; either in the de-industrialisation of North Wales (and much of the rest of a dis-United Kingdom) or in the steadfast dispatching of the Falklands Task Force. In the political economy of the poem, an infrastructure of elegy (in clear echo of the Scottish precursor Hamish Henderson's 'Elegies for the Dead in Cyrenaica', 1948) can but defer explorations of such bases as the close economic ties which have long, and tightly, bound Argentina to the UK. An exchange market of import and export is not to be confined to transferrable currencies of gold and silver, bank notes and coinage. The baser metals shuttle back and forth, too, whether in the form of railway lines or bullets. 'But what did it matter?' Steel in the heart (of Argentina). Or shrapnel?

Any unlayering of the Conran poem can be no less indicting in terms of ideologies. 'Doubtless he [Clifford Elley of Pontypridd] feasted' – but, when he is snatched from the valleys, into 'the presence of foes', 'the shadow [which] held him' was all too identifiable. Insignia of 'the staff and the fasces of tribunes' refer not only, directly, to the Roman imperial legacy of ever-westward conquest, but also, obliquely, to the General Staff and the Galtieri Fascism in which 'our virtue' has embroiled him. He, no less than the 'Phillip Sweet of Cwmback ... shy before girls', has been afforded little time to pass from a dance-hall dilatoriness of late adolescence to the rapid-fire *danse macabre* with the whores of death who now swoop over him and 'congregate like gulls on garbage'. No hint here of 'once more onto the breach', rather, as ever, onto the dump, unburied, dishonoured – 'under the air he is dead'. No Borges decorum of sleeping, eternally, with the enemy, beneath the snow, is given to these 'Gentlemen, all, from the streets and byways of Wales'. Their 'shroud is frost'.

Snow, frost ... 'the wind and the rain'. Will the poem come to rest elementally, leaving history to languish in the mists, and the myth, of inexplicable, unresolved time? Not so for Conran. A configuration of 'loose-fleshed whores', of 'Gentlemen', of 'honour', of 'steel in the heart', is denounced as but a figment. 'Empire/whore'... the signature is singular; and, unmistakable, the hand is that of the Iron Lady. The 'mead' of 1982 is the poisoned chalice of 'our [late imperialist] dregs'. Yet, however adamant, elemental, no regime survives forever. The Conran poem *performs* the song of the wind and the rain, not as 'my Lady's fool'. For, like the Shakespearean precursor it echoes, it is still the song of Feste, 'the wisest fool of all'.

Performing a song of the River Plate, one of Borges's last poems braves the iciest winter of a discontent, a prescience of death which invades even sleep, turning dream into nightmare. No decorum now, only certitude; and an immediacy which starkly identifies the bookish dreamer, through a subjective correlative, with the man-of-action. A younger Borges had often poeticised the ambivalent relation of literature to history in mock-heroic associations of writer-fighter. In the twilight of this late *milonga*,[13] an aged Borges engages directly, in the first person, with 'glacial isles' unnamed though unmistakable:

Milonga del muerto

Lo he soñado en esta casa
entre paredes y puertas.
Dios les permite a los hombres
soñar cosas que son ciertas.

Lo he soñado mar afuera
en unas islas glaciales.
Que nos digan lo demás
la tumba y los hospitales.

Una de tantas provincias
del interior fue su tierra.
(No conviene que se sepa
que muere gente en la guerra).

Lo sacaron del cuartel,
le pusieron en las manos
las armas y lo mandaron
a morir con sus hermanos.

Se obró con suma prudencia,
se habló de un modo prolijo.
Les entregaron a un tiempo
el rifle y el crucifijo.

Oyó las vanas arengas
de los vanos generales.
Vio lo que nunca había visto,
la sangre en los arenales.

Oyó vivas y oyó mueras,
oyó el clamor de la gente.
El sólo quería saber
si era o si no era valiente.

---

[13]   Borges, *Obras completas*, pp 497-8

Lo supo en aquel momento
en que le entraba la herida.
Se dijo No tuve miedo
cuando lo dejó la vida.

Su muerte fue una secreta
victoria. Nadie se asombre
de que me dé envidia y pena
el destino de aquel hombre.

Jorge Luis Borges

Milonga of the Dead Man

I have dreamed him in this house
amidst walls and doors.
God permits men
to dream things which are certain.

I dreamed him out at sea
on some glacial isles.
Let the tomb and hospitals
tell us the rest.

One of so many provinces
of the interior was his land.
(It is not proper that it be known
that people die in war.)

They took him out of the barracks,
They put in his hands
The weapons and they ordered
him to die with his brothers.

It was carried out with consummate prudence,
It was spoken with due propriety.
They gave him at the same time
The rifle and the crucifix.

He heard the vain harangues
of the vain generals.
He saw what he had never seen,
blood on the sands.

He heard shouts of 'Long live!' and 'Die!',
He heard the people's clamour.

He only wanted to know
if he was or wasn't brave.

He knew it the moment
the wound pierced him.
He said *I wasn't afraid*
when life left him.

His death was a secret
victory. Let no one wonder
that I feel envy and pity
at the fate of that man.

Jorge Luis Borges (my translation)

The tactic Borges indulges is that of rendering explicit, exemplifying, and then subverting, the conventionality of the genre of war poetry. By inserting into the *milonga* form what will emerge as a detailed narrative of a young soldier's rapid-fire translation from barracks to tomb via battlefield and hospital, his strategy is one of localising in an apparently sentimental style an easily performable song of regret. In the manner of 'Wo die Blumen noch sind?'/'Where Have All the Flowers Gone?', or 'Blowin' in the Wind', 'Milonga del muerto' assumes the simplest of popular song forms (in this case the even-verse assonanced octosyllabic quatrains of the traditional *porteño* lament with guitar accompaniment) whilst indulging both the generic protest and a rather more unusual formal ploy. As a poem (but not as a song) Borges's *milonga* can be seen (but not heard) to be constructed around a bracketed statement of the socially (im)permissible. The political expediency and the historical recording of wars in the late twentieth century are calculably informed by statistics of the number of body bags likely to be used in a given conflict. The impossibility of keeping the reality of death from the public has been highlighted in the Vietnam and, in high'tec vividness, the Gulf wars. 'Calculated acceptable losses', however, do not form part of what is disclosable in public or in private in this instance:

(No conviene que se sepa
que muere gente en la guerra.)

A *political* convention of keeping apart the military reality and the broadcast representations of heroic soldiering is parallelled by a *poetic* distancing effect. The opening insertion into a personal dream of an archetypal story of bravery and eventual death under fire is double-edged. The dream which is not a dream functions as a mode of indirection whereby the social convention or a political expediency of discretion in the reporting of war is almost at once to be blown apart ... not least by the ironically immediate *deus ex machina* dispensation which the poem's third and fourth lines permit in a Supreme Commander's 'lifting', as it were, 'of reporting restrictions'. What follows the crafty avoidance-of-censorship manoeuvre could hardly be a more stark, hardly a less restrained account of the cynical incompetence of 'the vain generals' of Argentina's misadventure in 'some glacial isles'. For six quatrains any niceties, any fuller hospital reports or tomb-stone inscriptions – let alone official versions – are set aside in favour of documented facts, preterite in tense and, in effect, getting over and done with that narrative which had entered the national imaginary and those necessary desires of the collective psyche. 'Worrying excess' in the 'getting back to history' is carefully reduced to a minimum, but that very minimum operates strongly as a supplement to dream. The poem ends by turning to effect the excess of yet another, always inadequate, narration of an individual's violent death, a catalogue of barracks-to-trench action familiar from Owen to Conran.

Borges is alert to and exploits a strain of anti-war lyric poetry comparable to that of Fernando Pessoa's unsentimental appropriation of Arthur Rimbaud's celebrated bathos of 'Le Dormeur du val' (1870).[14] Rimbaud's sonnet, it should be recalled, is constructed on a thirteen-line lulling into illusion whereby nature is made euphorically to cradle and protect the slumbering innocence of dreamy youth – before the fourteenth line's fatal revelation:

> Il a deux trous rouges au côté droit
> [He has two red holes in his right side]

Pessoa, in 'O menino da sua mãe' (1914?),[15] far from constructing his poem in parallel to the Rimbaud precursor, simply exploits its echo, and its final line, by inversion:

> No plaino abandonado
> Que a morna brisa aquece,
> De balas traspassado –
> Duas, de lado a lado –
> Jaz morto, e arrefece.

> On the abandoned plain
> Which the warm breeze heats,
> Shot through by bullets –
> Two, from side to side –
> He lies dead, and grows cold.

In this case, the distancing effect milked involves the boy-soldier's mother and wet nurse, locked in sentimental prayer for his safe and eternal return. They cannot know either of his already futile death or of their, and his, role in the

---

[14]   Arthur Rimbaud, *Selected Verse* (Harmondsworth. Penguin Books, 1962), p. 105-6.
[15]   Fernando Pessoa, *Poesia – 1 1902-1929*, *Obra Poética* (Lisbon: Publicaçoes Europa-América, 1987), pp 189-90.

ideology the poem lambasts:

> (Malhas que o Império tece!)
> [Webs the Empire weaves!]

Neither the Rimbaud nor the Pessoa poems performs a counter-narrative of the type which 'Milonga del Muerto' exploits, dialogically, from its opening line. With Borges, we can penetrate both the brackets and the intertext. It will be recalled that Juan López and John Ward were not allowed what I termed 'an infamous loss of particular identity whereby they are turned into 'The Unknown Soldier'. In the case of the *milonga*'s soldier, too, though he is unnamed, a relation of encounter without othering is subtly constructed. At the level of historical verisimilitude, the circumstances of his military service and premature death come to constitute a reality effect. But 'Lo he soñado'/'I have dreamed him' is an opening and, it should now be stressed, a closing device which situates the (inter)action on a psychic as much as on any specifically glacial, insular or other battlefield. The ethical restraint which informed Borges's technical distancing from Wilfred Owen's first-hand experience of combat is here dropped. In the circular ruins of his first-person dream-narrative, the poetic effect of self-other projection and identification is poignantly advanced in the last ten lines of the *milonga*. Up to this point, the dreamed conscript has been granted no attributes to distinguish him from other young provincial soldiers caught up in and brought down by vainglorious and pious discourses of 'el rifle y el crucifijo'. The device whereby he is given individuality is both ethical and literary, since recognition of his valour derives from the dreamer's projected desire and from an acclamation: 'and shall *I* face death without cowardice?'... *moriturus te saluto?* Many times, Jorge Luis Borges has revisited Argentine national identity in-the-making, whether linguistically, literarily or culturally, ever as an open, incomplete process.[16] The borrowing of characteristics from *porteño*, pampa or provincial differential histories might indeed have prepared his readers for the imprecation of the final quartet of 'Milonga del muerto':

> Nadie se asombre
> de que me dé envidia y pena
> el destino de aquel hombre

Insertion of a first-person voice operates as a reversion to a strategy which Borges had used in the early years of his poetic production (whether in the mode of 'Pienso en un tigre' or in the association of the self with a 'borrowed' heroic past). Here the process involves a prefiguration of the subject's own death whereby in sleep, on the vehicle of dream, the persona travels with the recruit to the glacial isles. The potentially excessive metaphor of a shared mortality is counter-balanced by the inseparability of 'pena'/'envidia', offering a particular

---

[16] See especially Borges's short collection *Para las seis cuerdas/For the Six Strings* of 1965. The first of the ten milongas, 'Milonga de los hermanos'/ 'Milonga of the two Brothers' ends on the Cain *versus* Abel note which 'Juan López y John Ward' carefully inverted.

re-reading of such a (standard) response to war (poetry). Here, heroism is embraced ... but with sad compassion. In a manner which anticipates my closing epigraph, I would suggest that the creative voice of the indelibly Argentine *milonga* seeks – not at all paradoxically – to break free of the limiting terms of the framing of national and personal identities. The dialogic relation of writer to fighter, revisited at the very end of Borges's life in the context of the recent Malvinas conflict, again challenges too easy assumptions regarding the interface of the making of history and the writing of its representation. There need be no wonderment at the treatment of the complex interplay of 'envidia y pena' if we recall the strategic mode whereby the poem of the two Johns dealt with the (un)translatability of a *mediated* self-other relationship. Again, in this *milonga*, the writing operates in excess of a soulful lament; in excess of both self-identification with and difference from the other. Again, a poem resists making capital ... in this instance, out of *Nation*.

Returning to questions of cultural difference and of excess, the seemingly restrained discourse of Jorge Luis Borges, responding both to such European precursors as Wilfred Owen and Fernando Pessoa and to certain Argentine canons of literariness, can be said to construe the particularity of any national culture as indissociable from a capacity to read; to read the other as a function of the ability resistantly to read the self. The Susana Thénon and Tony Conran poems are differently excessive. Thénon's rhetoric affronts conservative Argentine good taste. Conran's might just do the same in the United Kingdom ... were little Englanders ever to read him.[17] But strange meetings do, occasionally, occur. My title struggles to propose that it is often necessary to translate not only *between* but also *within* cultures; to wage war *in* poetry. What kind of conflict would such poetry be? I shall cede the word not to Owen or to Borges, not to Thénon or to Conran, but to a Jamaican, explaining what he calls a 'war of position' from inside a United Kingdom still striving to come to terms – and to texts – with the multicultural but by no means simultaneous *trans*nation within:

A 'war of position' is where you advance on a number of different positions at once ... through those sites like the culture, moral and social questions, the

---

[17]   I am indebted to Dr Peter Kitson and Dr Tony Brown of The University of Wales, Bangor, for providing me access to that critical community of Welsh writers which has responded to the work of Tony Conran. In his '"Shaman of shifting form": Tony Conran and Welsh *barddas*', the poet M. Wynne Thomas suggests that 'Conran's greatest success in this "freer" mode ... is probably his elegy (or synthetic *awdl*) for the Welsh soldiers who died at Bluff Cove'. He devotes but two telling pages to the poem, and concludes: 'The Welsh are appropriately among the last to fall victim to that vision of British Empire to which they have so eagerly subscribed ever since Tudor times, suppressing in the process all memory of their own separate history, that stretches back to the period of the *Gododdin* His own remittingly dark elegy brings Aneirin's ancient poem tangentially to bear on the Welsh present, to powerful tragic effect The young soldiers (addressed as "Gentlemen all", in a quintessentially English turn of phrase used here with a combination of irony and sincerity) are represented as the victims not only of Margaret Thatcher's aggressive chauvinism but also of a Welsh "nation" culpably besotted with the Britishness that has left it economically devastated ("Aberdare, Denbigh and Neath"), fertile ground for military recruitment". M Wynne Thomas in, *Thirteen Ways of Looking at Tony Conran*, edited by Nigel Jenkins (Cardiff, Welsh Union of Writers, 1995), pp. 98-9.

family, education, religion, gender, sexuality, race, national identity, the media, religion, which the new social movements and the 'culturing of politics' have brought into the centre of the political equation ... The real break comes not from inverting the model but from breaking free of its limiting terms, changing the frame.

Stuart Hall

CHAPTER 8

The Transmission of Science from Europe to Argentina and its Impact on Literature: from Lugones to Borges

Eduardo L. Ortiz*

In the fifty years from 1870 to 1920 Argentina's literary circles were deeply influenced by current trends in the international scene which, as in any peripheral country, were listened to attentively. However, there were also endogenous influences. The rapid development of science and technology and its much wider public understanding in Argentina were among them. This chapter explores interactions between the literary and the scientific communities of Argentina in that period. The background which made possible a fairly fluid and perhaps fruitful interaction between these two communities is discussed from the standpoint of the history of the exact sciences in Argentina.

The special communication that existed between the communities of scientists, writers and poets in Argentina from the 1870s contributed to enhance these exchanges. This link has deep historical roots. Argentina was a society in which literature and poetry occupied the higher echelons of culture; however, an earlier perception of science as a vehicle of progress and liberation played a substantial role in its acceptance. This particular understanding of science was first introduced in Argentina at the time of the struggles for independence, when the idea of science as a necessary instrument to build a new nation was first proposed at government level. This perception reverberated well into the present century. It has also evoked, until fairly recent times, an obscure response in some circles of power in Argentina which, for the same reasons, understood science as inherently subversive.

The chapter begins with a sketch of the understanding of problems related to infinity, space, time and matter in Buenos Aires at the end of the nineteenth and the beginning of the twentieth centuries. Specialist scientific circles and educated general audiences are discussed in parallel. Because of the particular impact of some specific topics on literature, such as the theory of relativity and Cantor's ideas on the theory of infinity, their transmission from Europe to Argentina is considered here in more detail than can be found in works on the history of science in Argentina.

A very brief reference is made to the background of reform and modernisation, which characterised academic life in Argentina in the early years

* I wish to thank Evelyn Fishburn for many discussions which stimulated my interest in this topic and the John Simon Guggenheim Memorial Foundation, New York, for its support while this paper was being written

of this century, particularly in the late 1910s and early 1920s, and of the role assigned to science by these reformers. In many respects, this period was a turning point in the cultural life of Argentina for both science and literature.

The second part of the chapter revolves around Albert Einstein's visit to Argentina in 1925,[1] in which the poet Leopoldo Lugones played a key role. The impact of this visit exceeded the boundaries of pure science. It brought to a much larger audience the discussion of questions related to the structure of space, time, matter, radiation, infinity, and the absolute and relative.

These discussions echoed strongly in Argentina's literary and philosophical circles. One can detect an interesting change in the use of scientific imagery in Argentine literature after the 1920s, which seems to correlate with two very specific and radically different periods in the reception of some of the main contemporary ideas in mathematics, physics and astronomy in that country. The choice of models for their imagery marks a profound break between Lugones and younger writers, such as Borges, who were also interested in the broader implications of the exact sciences. While the first used an imagery grounded in sound and light, Borges experimented with an imagery more closely related to the paradoxes of infinity, fragmented time and the unusual spaces brought about by modern physics, which were not directly connected with our intuitive reality.

Some foreign bibliography on modern mathematics and physics available to the educated non-specialist public in Argentina in the 1930s and 1940s is included. Finally, the use Borges made of some objects and ideas related to modern mathematics and physics is briefly considered in the third part of the chapter.

Space, time, matter and infinity in Argentina: 1890-1920: Some remarks on stages in the transmission of science to Argentina

The archaeology of the transmission of science to Argentina reveals significantly different strata. Some of these strata continued echoing long after their time and their influence was often modified or reinforced by subsequent acquisitions. The vitality of the intellectual impact of some of these different layers can be judged not only by their relative permanence in scientific circles,[2] but also by their permanence in non-scientific intellectual circles.

A basic layer records, through Spanish sources, the transmission of

---

[1]   For details on Einstein's visit to Argentina see E. L. Ortiz, 'A convergence of interests. Einstein's visit to Argentina in 1925', *Ibero-Amerkanisches Archiv*, vol. 21, nos 1/2, Berlin (1995), pp. 67-126.
[2]   The ideas of some of the French Idéologues, such as Cabanis and Destutt de Tracy, continued to have a vital impact and to be invoked by scientists in Argentina as well as in Spain until the end of the First World War This was particularly true in physiology, an area of research in which scientists of both countries received Nobel awards

seventeenth-century science such as the work of Kircher and Caramuel.[3] A strong mark was left by the controversies between Jansenists and Jesuits and the beginnings of the philosophical doctrine of probabilism. The latter maintained that certainty was unattainable outside the formal sciences and that probability was the only available guide. These ideas mixed with older inheritances, in particular the hermetic thought of Raimundo Llull. In this stratum the magic of numbers, the powerful art of combinations, and the mysterious connections between symbols, words and objects played a leading role. This layer was the substratum on which rested the message of the French Philosophers: the need for a shift from deep metaphysical problems to those which would materially benefit human society. These ideas were transmitted to Argentina from Spain in the late Colonial period with selective emphasis. They were followed in the early nineteenth century by those of the French 'Idéologie' school, whose impact was extraordinary. This school emphasised collection, classification, ordering and analysis, and the construction of a science of ideas. At the time of Independence, the teachings of the Idéologie, often through local interpretations, were the philosophical dynamo behind the foundation of the main cultural institutions of Argentina: from the college of moral sciences and the university to the national collections, that is, the national library and the museums.[4] *Ideología* became a synonym of philosophy in advanced university education.

The philosophical background to late nineteenth-century science cannot be exhausted through the traditional references to French positivism; though, no doubt, it was an important element in it. Positivism is not enough to characterise this complex period, as it offers a picture of science in Argentina in which entire areas are shadowed, some of which are essential to the topic of this chapter. In particular, it belittles a serious interest in metaphysical problems which developed among exact scientists in Argentina in the 1880s; for example, a concern with the understanding of space, time and infinity.

In the late 1880s, Valentín Balbín,[5] the leading mathematician of nineteenth-century Argentina, ran an advanced seminar on mathematical physics at the Sociedad Científica Argentina, which was then the main scientific society in the country. Balbín was assisted by his friend Jorge Duclout, a distinguished physicist and engineer of French origin, a graduate of Zürich Polytechnikum. One of the central concerns of their seminar was the foundations of geometry and the understanding of space. Duclout's substantial lectures on these topics were published in the journal of the Sociedad Científica in the early 1890s.[6] A few years earlier Balbín published in Buenos Aires a treatise on an abstract algebra (the so-called theory of quaternions) due to William Hamilton. Unlike

---

[3]   Atanasio Kircher, 1602-80. Juan Caramuel, 1606-82.

[4]   The same could be said of other countries of North and South America.

[5]   E. L. Ortiz, 'El contexto Europeo de la revista matemática de Valentín Balbín: 1889-1892', in M. de Asúa (ed), *Perspectivas históricas de la ciencia en Argentina* (Buenos Aires: Centro Editor de América Latina, 1993), pp. 86-109.

[6]   J Duclout, 'Los fundamentos de la geometría y el conocimiento del espacio', *Anales de la Sociedad Científica Argentina* (Buenos Aires, 1890-91)

traditional algebra, its elements are not numbers but four dimensional entities of far greater generality. Generalisations of this new algebra played a role in the formulation of the theory of relativity twenty years later.

The work of Georg Cantor and Richard Dedekind on the mathematical theory of infinity, developed in the last quarter of the nineteenth century, attempted to give an answer to old and difficult problems which were at the roots of science. They had been raised already by Zeno, of the Eleatic school, and were revisited again and again through the ages. Nicholas de Cusa and later Galileo Galilei[7] made deep contributions to their understanding, but without finding definite answers. As is well known,[8] Cantor and Dedekind approached the problem from different viewpoints and both contributed original ideas. Their work allowed mathematical thought to penetrate into an entirely new province: the theory of infinity. One point of departure for this theory was the acceptance that a set of elements can be coordinated element to element with a part of it, if it has an infinite number of elements.[9]

The new mathematical physics, in which space, time and very rapid movement became central concerns, reached Argentina in the early years of this century. In 1909 a well endowed Physics Institute was created at the new University of La Plata, and distinguished German professors were imported to run it. One of them had been the first scientist to write a paper in collaboration with Albert Einstein.

The questions of space and time and also of infinity were discussed in the 1901 doctoral dissertation of the young mathematician Claro Cornelio Dassen.[10] The third chapter of his work is devoted to the discussion of arguments involving infinity, which lead to contradictions called paradoxes of infinity.[11] His work attracted the attention of the logicians Louis Couturat and Bertrand Russell.

The end of the First World War signalled the beginning of a time of change in the world and also in Argentina, whose universities began to be updated after the so-called Reforma Universitaria of 1918. This was a serious student revolt

---

[7]   In his *Discursi e dimostrazione matematique in torno a due nouve scienze*, he stated that the relations of equality, greater and smaller apply only to finite quantities

[8]   For a perspective of Cantor and Dedekind's classic work, viewed from a modern standpoint, see the recent book of D Goldrei, *Classic set theory a guided independent study* (London: Chapman & Hall, 1996).

[9]   This assumption takes into account, for example, that the elements of the infinite sequence of integers 1, 2, 3, 4,   can be associated, term by term, with the infinite sequence of even numbers, which is a part of it.

[10]   C C Dassen, *Metafísica de los conceptos matemáticos fundamentales (espacio, tiempo, cantidad, límite) y del llamado análisis infinitesimal* (Buenos Aires: Tailhade & Rosselli, 1901)

[11]   Logical paradoxes have a long history in the Spanish language; Cervantes used them in *Don Quixote*. In the Second Part, Chapter II, Cervantes made reference to the following paradox. the owner of a bridge stated that anyone wishing to cross it must declare where is he going. If his statement was untrue, he would be hanged A traveller states he wishes to cross as he is to be hanged on the other side of the river

which had echoes in a good part of Latin America. The 1920s was also the decade of José Ingenieros's *Revista de Filosofía*,[12] a journal which attempted to establish bridges between science and philosophy. Questions about space and time, and also about Einstein's relativity, appeared often in the pages of this journal. The progressive literary journal *Nosotros* was also interested in these questions, and published a long expository paper on the theory of relativity in 1923.

In the 1920s advance was not limited to modernisation through the import of new facts or theories. Towards the end of the decade it was possible to detect signs showing that the scientific communities were beginning to be reorganised along more modern lines. Patterns of hierarchy were being dictated then, more strongly than before, by the internal evaluation of peers rather than by the views of patrons or consumers of their activities. On the literary side, Borges and other young literary figures of the time became, gradually, more concerned with the views of other poets[13] rather than with the resonance their work might find in contemporaneous social or political movements.

The Spanish mathematician Julio Rey Pastor received his training in Germany; he was also an exceptional lecturer with a wide cultural background. Rey Pastor visited Argentina in 1917 and subsequently settled there permanently. He was a decisive factor in the reception of Cantor's ideas in Argentina. In 1917 he gave advanced seminars on mathematics in Buenos Aires but, in addition, he offered a series of lectures on the contemporaneous crisis in, and reconstruction of, mathematics. His topic attracted an audience beyond the professional mathematician.[14] The central theme of the lectures was Cantor's theory of sets and its role in the reconstruction of mathematics. He began his lectures with a challenging statement: 'If somebody would ask me for a definition of Mathematics, I would say that it will become the Science of Sets'. He proved to be right. Through the 1920s Rey Pastor's articles in the newspaper *La Nación* contributed to the public understanding of infinity, the new conceptions of geometry, space-time and relativity.

This was, in general terms, the position of space, time and infinity in the early 1920s in Argentina in both the small circle of specialists and in the larger scenario of cultural Buenos Aires. The process of the transmission of Cantor's ideas to Argentina's scientific community can be regarded as having been completed when Borges, in his early twenties, was back in his country.

---

[12]   The collection of *Revista de Filosofía* (1915-29) is published by The Humboldt Library, Sources for the History of Science and Culture in Portugal, Spain and Latin America (London: Imperial College, 1998) with an introduction by E. L. Ortiz

[13]   Borges's attitude towards Breton and his Manifest is an example of this. See E. Rodríguez Monegal, *Jorge Luis Borges A Literary Biography* (New York· Dutton, 1978), pp. 301-2.

[14]   On Rey Pastor see E. L. Ortiz, 'Prologue', in Vol. I of *The Works of Julio Rey Pastor*, Vols. I-VIII (London· The Humboldt Library, 1988). His lectures were published in book form under the title of. *Introducción a la Matemática Superior* (Madrid. Biblioteca Corona, 1916); a reprint with an introduction by E. L. Ortiz was published by the Instituto de Estudios Riojanos in Logroño, in 1988 They are reproduced in his *Works*, Vol. I, MF 1916: 18-20, 1988.

Poets, writers and scientists in late nineteenth- and early twentieth-century Argentina

Holmberg, Lugones and Borges

Kroeber[15] has indicated that science fiction appears when the supernatural is driven out of enlightened society. Instead of looking for magic, writers extrapolate the consequences of the same scientific and technological advances that are driving superstition out. In these periods one can sense a desire for the anticipation of ideas and results which are not yet within the domain of science, but which can be grasped through literature or poetry.

A clear example of this can be found in the works of the Argentine writer Eduardo L. Holmberg. He wrote crime fiction stories and introduced an overlap of scientific, spiritualist and fantastic literature to his country in the 1870s. Holmberg is regarded by leading experts on the history of literature in Argentina, such as Ricardo Rojas, as the founder of fantastic literature in his country. He was not only a fine writer, but also one of the most influential scientists in the second half of nineteenth-century Argentina. Holmberg, a committed Darwinist, was the most vocal fighter against superstition of his generation.[16]

However, he was neither the first nor the only scientist with a solid literary name in Argentina. Carlos Encina, a distinguished poet, was also a scientist: a professor and later dean of the Mathematics Faculty of Buenos Aires University;[17] the leading Argentine writers Vicente López and Juan María Gutiérrez had also received training in the exact sciences. There were also distinguished writers with an active professional life in the field of medicine; Dr. Eduardo Wilde was perhaps the most celebrated among them.

Towards the end of the century, through the influence of Holmberg and other scientists, there was a deep intertwining of the scientific and literary communities in Argentina. This was a time when science was, worldwide, a source of inspiration to poets and writers. Modernists, such as Rubén Darío and Leopoldo Lugones, were warmly received in the *tertulias* of the scientists. Their views were found to have much in common with the scientist's ethos of the time. As a journalist, young Lugones often reported on new scientific advances achieved both abroad and in Argentina.

In his fictional writing of the late 1890s Lugones made much use of science, far more than Borges would ever do. Several of the stories later collected in *Las*

---

[15]   K. Kroeber, *Romantic Fantasy and Science Fiction* (New Haven and London: Yale University Press, 1988)

[16]   However, it would not be right to classify Holmberg as a follower of Spencer's social Darwinism; see E. L. Ortiz, 'La inserción de la ciencia moderna en Argentina', closing address to the Congress of the Sociedad Española de Historia de la Ciencia, *Actas*, vol I (Madrid: Sociedad Española de Historia de la Ciencia, 1984), pp. 89-108

[17]   His early poetical work and his 'Canto al Arte', of 1877, show the influence of science.

fuerzas extrañas [Strange Forces][18] were written in these years. In a story published in the newspaper Tribuna, with the title 'La biblioteca infernal' [The Infernal Library],[19] Lugones revisited the old theme of a journey into a fantastic library. He wrote about a book, the last page of which was 'un postigo abierto sobre la inmensidad' [a shutter opening on to immensity]. In this and other stories Lugones mixed contemporaneous European influences with elements drawn from the seventeenth-century Kircherian strata received by Argentina from Spain.

The poet Leopoldo Lugones and the public understanding of the theory of relativity in Argentina

In 1920 the poet Leopoldo Lugones was invited by the Faculty of Sciences of Buenos Aires University to deliver a lecture on Einstein's theory of relativity. For nearly a year, relativity had been attracting a great deal of public attention in Europe and also in Argentina. A commission, sponsored by the Royal Society and headed by the physicist Arthur Stanley Eddington, had verified astronomical implications of that theory in 1919.

Lugones's lecture was subsequently published in the form of a small book: *El tamaño del espacio* [The Extent of Space]. This booklet is not yet another popular exposition of relativity. It is much more than that: it is a presentation of the new theory through the eyes of a poet with immense imagination. Clearly *El tamaño del espacio* has serious flaws and nobody would have learned the details of the theory of relativity through it. However, his lecture is especially relevant to the history of ideas in Argentina in the first half of our century. This is because Lugones, then at the pinnacle of his fame, accorded relativity theory a status in Argentina which went beyond newspaper sensationalism. Through his lecture he managed to put the question of the interplay between space, time, matter and radiation in a uniquely favourable setting for the audiences of cultured Buenos Aires, this was a far more important factor for the public reception there of relativity, and of its philosophical implications, than the precision of his physics. His lecture also gave a serious boost to modern mathematics and mathematical physics in the eyes of the educated general public. With Lugones the trend reversed itself in Argentina, and literature began to have an influence on the development of science.

After Lugones's 1920 piece, interest in Einstein's theories was encouraged by the publication of translations of popular explanations and also by local works. By mid-1922, serious efforts began to be made to bring Einstein to Argentina. One year later, details of his visit had been formalised. Lugones was by then one of the few Argentines Einstein could clearly place. They met in Geneva early in 1925 as delegates to the Commission of Intellectual

---

[18] L. Lugones, *Las fuerzas extrañas* (Buenos Aires: M. Gleizer, 1906)

[19] *Tribuna*, Buenos Aires, February 14, 1899. (P. L Barcia, introduction, L. Lugones, *Cuentos fantásticos* (Madrid: Castalia, 1987), gives 17 December 1898 as the date of publication of this story).

Cooperation of the League of Nations, to which both were elected simultaneously. Lugones was saluted there as one of the main contemporary poets in the Spanish language. He remained the central character in the story of Einstein's visit to Argentina: all threads converged in him.

Einstein's visit to Argentina took place in March-April 1925; sadly, it took place too late in time. His pacifist and internationalist views of world affairs were not as attractive in the Argentina of 1925 as they had been when he was given an honorary degree by the University of Buenos Aires three years earlier. The changes that had taken place in Argentina and indeed in the world within these few years also affected his own areas of contact with Argentine culture. Even his friend Lugones had already begun an ideological transition in the critical period of 1923-25, moving steadily towards the political right.

Nevertheless, Einstein's visit had a considerable impact, and it acted as a catalyst in a number of intellectual concerns which had been brewing in Argentina since the end of the First World War. This impact was not only felt in science, but also in philosophy. At the time, positivism, or rather, a local interpretation of scientism with elements of positivism, was under siege by a group of philosophers who emphasised a return to Kant and closer links with contemporaneous German philosophy. Coriolano Alberini, as one of the leaders of those who favoured this trend, interpreted Einstein's views as the ultimate rejection of positivism. Alberini was also moving steadily in the direction of Italian fascism in these years. It is ironic that Einstein's more immediate entourage while in Argentina would soon be moving to support (or were already on the way to supporting) political systems he publicly rejected. Einstein's movements in Argentina were closely guarded by his local mentors, perhaps afraid of his tendency to speak his mind. Although José Ingenieros had been very active in canvassing for Einstein's visit to Argentina, on scientific as well as on philosophical grounds, his group did not receive much of Einstein's attention.

In the first half of the 1920s, one can also detect in Argentina's literary and artistic circles a concern with the possible implications of Einstein's ideas. The years immediately before the physicist's visit was a period of intense change, when modernism[20] in poetry, championed among others by Lugones, was being challenged by ultraism. The concern of the young Argentine poets and writers of that generation with problems of infinity, space and time took a new turn, which would be more fully expressed in their work following the 1920s decade. No doubt foreign influences, through readings or visits abroad, acted upon them, but it seems equally clear that the intense and wide debate generated by Einstein's presence contributed to focus such concerns.

---

[20]   On modernism in the River Plate see A. Zum Felde, *El proceso intelectual del Uruguay*, vol. II, 5th ed. (Montevideo: Librosur, 1987) and also C A. Loprete, *La literatura modernista en la Argentina* (Buenos Aires. Editorial Poseidon, 1955)

In their attitudes towards science and the supernatural there was extensive common ground between modernists and ultraists. If, however, we follow Gerald Holton's[21] characterisation of Einstein's conceptions as a search for a world picture which encompasses all phenomena, as a quest for unification which necessarily implies the breaking of barriers,[22] we may place ultraists slightly closer than modernists to a perception of reality compatible with Einstein's conceptions.

Concern with space and time and algebraic metaphors was expressed by Jorge Luis Borges in a poem he placed in time in 1922:[23]

> *Silenciosas batallas del ocaso*
> *en arrabales últimos,*
> *siempre antiguas derrotas*
> *de una guerra en el cielo,*
> *albas ruinosas que nos llegan*
> *desde el fondo del espacio*
> *como desde el fondo del tiempo*

> Soundless battles of sunset
> beyond the ragged edges of the city
> the ancient recurring defeats of a war in heaven, ruinous
> white
> dawns that come for us
> out of the empty ends of space
> as from the ends of time ....

and later

> *soy yo esas cosas y las otras*
> *o son llaves secretas y árduas álgebras*
> *de lo que no sabremos nunca?*

> am I these things, and others,
> or are they secret keys, impossible algebras
> of what we shall never know?

---

[21]   See G Holton, 'Cultural roots of modern science Einstein's "Rebellion"', Rothschild Distinguished Lecture, Harvard University, 6 May 1997, to be published by Harvard University.

[22]   Such as the frontiers between the traditional concepts of matter and energy; space and time; or fluctuations in the microscopic and in the observable.

[23]   J. L. Borges, 'Líneas que pude haber escrito y perdido hacia 1922' in *Obra poética* (Madrid: Alianza, 1972), p. 54. ['Lines I Might Have Written And Lost Around 1922', *Jorge Luis Borges Selected Poems 1923-1967* (London: Allen Lane-The Penguin Press, p. 229).] Borges was also exposed to the interest relativity theory aroused in Europe while he lived there, until 1924. Einstein visited Spain in 1923; on this visit see T F Glick, *Einstein y los españoles, ciencia y sociedad en la España de entreguerras* (Madrid: Alianza, 1986)

If a poetic and literary view of science is an important part of Lugones's legacy, it seems clear that the scientific imagery he handled: heat, light and sound (cum spiritualism), was more realistic, tangible and concrete than the abstractions used by Borges in the 1930s and 1940s. Borges's fiction manipulated a world of dislocated time, new geometric objects, space-time games and geometric stories. I would say that this difference, *son et lumière* vs. time and infinity, marks a substantial division between the two writers, perhaps deeper than the differences between the literary schools to which each of them adhered.

In the 1930s and early 1940s several substantial Argentine writers were using the imagery of science in their writings. One of them was Roberto Arlt. He gave a literary dimension to the fascinating personality of physicist Teobaldo J. Ricaldoni, one of the founders of physics research in Argentina, who fitted the popular image of the mad, obsessive inventor. In some of his stories Arlt referred to Ricaldoni, both by name and by description. Arlt, however, used an 'industrial-scientific' imagery which, in its contents, had more in common with that of Lugones than with the abstract imagery Borges used in his fiction.

Two other important literary works in which the imagery of science plays an important role were produced between the end of the 1930s and the beginning of the 1940s. One of them is Adolfo Bioy Casares's *La invención de Morel* [The Invention of Morel], an early exploration into virtual reality.[24] Like Borges, his friend, Bioy Casares did not have formal training in science, but he did have a genuine interest in it. The other important work is Ernesto Sábato's collection of short essays, *Uno y el Universo* [One and the Universe].[25] The author was a physics graduate from the University of La Plata, where he later gained a doctorate in experimental physics. He made interesting remarks in this work about Borges's 'geometric' crime fiction; we will return to this point later.

We have just sketched out the process of the transmission of some of the main ideas related to space, time, infinity and relativity to the large educated audiences of Argentina. In addition to local articles and general books on mathematics and modern physics, there were foreign sources available to a non-specialist audience in Argentina in the 1920s and 1930s. I shall now review briefly some of these sources.

Borges has generously given concrete references to this literature in his fictional work. In *La doctrina de los ciclos,*[26] written in 1934, he gave a number of references to foreign scientific literature he read while writing this story. He acknowledged the use of Bertrand Russell's books *Introduction to Mathematical Philosophy*[27] and *The ABC of Atoms*[28] and of Arthur S. Eddington's *The Nature*

---

[24]   A. Bioy Casares, *La invención de Morel* (Buenos Aires: Emecé, 1956).

[25]   E Sábato, *Uno y el Universo* (Buenos Aires: Editorial Sudoamericana, 1968).

[26]   J L. Borges, *Historia de la eternidad* (Buenos Aires: Emecé, 1953).

[27]   Published in London in 1919. This work was reviewed in *Revista de Filosofía* in July 1920, p. 145 There were numerous references to Russell and his work around 1920 in this journal.

of the Physical World.[29] Russell's *The Study of Mathematics*, initially published in November 1907 in *The New Quarterly* and later reproduced in *Mysticism and Logic*, was read and discussed in intellectual circles in Argentina in the 1920s, mainly through its French translation of 1922.[30] Russell made in it a brief but brilliant evaluation of Cantor's work.

Other substantial sources Borges may have read in English before 1934 are: Tobias Dantzig's *Number, The Language of Science*,[31] originally published in 1930, and E. T. Bell's *Men of Mathematics*, also from 1930. Both books were translated into Spanish and published in Argentina in the mid 1940s. Dantzig's was published by Librería del Colegio in 1947 and Bell's by Editorial Losada. It should be noted that Borges became a member of the board of Losada's publishing house. Both books contain chapters on Cantor's work and on the magical fascination of numbers; they are still regarded as masterful accounts.

Borges was well acquainted with another important work of the period, *Mathematics and the Imagination*, of E. Kasner and J. Newman,[32] a book remarkable for the clarity of its concepts and for the originality of the exposition. Borges wrote a review of it and declared it to be one of those very special books he would read again and again and cover with manuscript notes.[33]

Mathematical and physical imagery in the fictional work of Jorge Luis Borges

Playing with strange geometrical objects

Some remarks will now be made on some of the mathematical imagery used by Borges in his fictional work. The ideas he used concern mainly language, infinity, strange geometrical objects in which infinity played a central role, probability, combinatorial games and, also, a genre which could be called the 'geometric' novel. In the process of incorporating them into his fiction, Borges metamorphosed these ideas and, occasionally, enriched their extra-scientific dimension.

'La Biblioteca de Babel' ['The Library of Babel'][34] is a story with a definite taste of Swift. It is reminiscent of Lugones's 'La biblioteca infernal' ['The Infernal Library'], but goes far beyond it. It has a special interest in that it combines most of the mathematical imagery mentioned before. Clearly, the

---

[28]   B Russell, *The ABC of Atoms* (London: K. Paul, Trench, Trubuer, 1923).

[29]   A.S. Eddington, *The Nature of the Physical World* (London and Cambridge: Cambridge University Press, 1928).

[30]   B. Russell, *Le Mysticisme et la logique* (Paris: Payot, 1922).

[31]   London: Macmillan, 1930; with new editions in 1933 and 1939.

[32]   Published in New York by Simon and Schuster in 1940.

[33]   These three books were published in the USA and were written by mathematicians of US origin or living in the USA.

[34]   Borges, *Ficciones* (Buenos Aires· Emecé, 1956).

library is a model of the universe. It has been generated through the combinations of a finite number of 'atomic' signs: letters spaces and punctuation. One of the volumes is deciphered and found to contain notions of combinatorial analysis illustrated with examples of variations with unlimited repetition;[35] this last notion is necessary to relieve the library from being trivially finite. With this new notion a gifted librarian is able to discover the fundamental laws of the library. After the experimental verification[36] that no two books in the library are identical he is able to deduce that the library is total; that is, it contains all that can be expressed in any language. His discovery is received with joy, but it is soon realised that truth is as inaccessible as before: the probability of finding in this infinitude a given vindication, a prophesy of one's life, is nearly zero.

The story comes closest to Swift[37] when Borges describes a sect preaching the suspension of searches and a redirection of all efforts to reshuffling symbols until truth is found. Again these wishes are confounded by the laws of probability, as the probability of such an event is close to zero. Another direction of searches is to look for just one book, a compendium of all books, which could be a shortcut to truth. The small probability of actually finding the required item in the library destroys, again, all hopes. The library, like Funes's memory,[38] is all storage, with no intelligence, structure or soul to make selective retrieval possible.

This point in Borges seems to me to be of some interest in view of the archaeology we have described for the transmission of European science to Argentina. As has been said, the Idéologues, approach dominated science for a very considerable period there, starting at the time of Independence[39] and still detectable as a dynamic force over a century later. This school had a conception of the role of science which is not contradictory to the one used by the characters in this story of Borges. For the Idéologues science was essentially an exercise in classification:[40] its main objective was to order and classify sensorial information and, if possible, find a system of signs capable of describing it, that is, to construct its language. Analogously, similar languages were actually constructed for several areas of science and technology, for example, for plants (by Linnaeus), for machines (by Lanz),[41] for chemical compounds (by Lavoisier). The decimal system for the classification of books was also first proposed in this

---

[35] ' ..nociones de análisis combinatorio, ilustradas por ejemplos de variaciones con repetición ilimitada'
[36] As with the theory of relativity in 1919, this experiment brings a connection to reality.
[37] A similar scene takes place in J. Swift, *Gulliver's Travels*, 1726, Part II, Chapter V; it was a parody of the recently founded Royal Society, London's academy of sciences.
[38] J. L Borges, 'Funes el memorioso', in *Ficciones*.
[39] Through the teachings of Borges's ancestor Juan Crisóstomo Lafinur (1797-1824).
[40] Thus their emphasis on collections and museums.
[41] Lanz had a fascinating personality both as a man and as a scientist; he visited Argentina in 1816-17 and advised the government on the reorganisation of studies of advanced mathematics there along modern European models; see Ortiz, E. L. and Bret, P. 'José María de Lanz and the Paris-Cadiz axis', *Cahiers d'Histoire et de Philosophie des Sciences*, Paris (1998).

period. Interest in the development of languages for blind persons and for people
with other disabilities date from the same period; some of these efforts are
related to the work of members of the French Idéologues.

However, Condorcet, who was one of the contributors and also a sharp critic
of this extensive project, observed in 1780 that classification leads to a
multiplication of levels which increases exponentially, making the probability of
finding any specific item in it arbitrarily small. This is essentially the point
Borges revisited in this story.[42] A footnote at the end of the story says that it had
been pointed out to the author that an infinite library is not necessary; it could be
replaced by a single book with an infinite number of pages. Its pages would be
like thin slices of a solid. Borges associates this formulation of his story with
Cavalieri's principle, a mathematics favourite when he was a student. This
seventeenth-century topic of pre-infinitesimal calculus was used until recently in
the teaching of solid geometry. Cavalieri assumed that solids could be imagined
as being made up of thin plane layers, like sheets of paper, which can be
displaced one over the other to produce differently shaped polyhedral bodies,
but leaving the volume unchanged.[43]

For his book with an infinite number of pages Borges referred to the idea of
the density of real numbers, that is, to the concept that in between two real
numbers it is always possible to insert another one.

The same geometric object is revisited in 'El libro de arena' ['The Book of
Sand'],[44] where the author buys a diabolical book with an infinite number of thin
pages which obsesses him with its eternal novelty:[45] for reasons of probability,
what he has seen once cannot be found again. He dropped the book, wisely, on a
shelf in the cellar of the old Argentine National Library, where the maps and
periodicals collection was stored and was slowly consumed by dampness.
Geometrical objects of a simpler structure appear in other stories; in 'El disco'
['The Disc'] Borges deals with a one sided circle,[46] a sort of impossible Moebius
band. Questions such as curves which can cover an area in the plane or infinite
self-similar constructions (now called fractal structures), were available in
Argentina through Rey Pastor's works,[47] but do not seem to have found their
way into literature in these years.

---

[42]   In another story published three years later, 'Tema del traidor y del héroe' (*Artificios*, 1944),
Borges made an explicit reference to Condorcet's decimal system of classification.
[43]   Bonaventura Cavalieri, 1598-1647, was a gifted student of Galileo His work is a foundation
for the invention of infinitesimal calculus.
[44]   'El libro de arena', in J L. Borges, *El libro de arena* (Buenos Aires: Emecé, 1975). In this
story and in some of his poetry, sand plays the double role of measurer of time and a sample of an
infinitely large number of objects.
[45]   Borges says. 'porque ni el libro ni la arena tienen ni principio ni fin' [because neithe the book
nor the sand has any beginning or end (*The Book of Sand*, Harmondsworth: Penguin Books, 1979,
p. 89)]. Borges postulates, unnecessarily, that in this book no page is the first or the last.
[46]   He says in the Epílogo: 'es el círculo euclidiano' [the Euclidean Circle].
[47]   Rey Pastor referred to this question in the discussion of the notion of curve and dimension in
his *Introducción a la Matemática Superior*

Recursion, fix points and the eternal return

Infinity is reconsidered in *La doctrina de los ciclos*,[48] which contains a direct reference to Cantor's work and to the fact that, even if rational numbers, the vulgar fractions,[49] can be put into a one-to-one correspondence with integer numbers, this is done at the expense of breaking order.[50] Borges recalls that the same thing happens to ordinality if points in the plane are mapped on the real line. Here he makes a brief but interesting remark, associating points in space with time. 'La serie de los puntos del espacio (o de los instantes del tiempo) no es ordenable así' [that is, well ordered, with a well defined predecessor and follower for each given number]. This cryptic remark may be a reference to the space-time plane. The theory of relativity does not assign to time a line direction, a ray, as classical physics does. It mixes space and time into a single structure in which the classically ordered sequence of events is disturbed. In this sense one could say that after and before lose their traditional meanings.

Borges played again with infinity in this essay when he introduced the idea of the eternal return, which he discussed in Nietzsche's version: as the number of atoms, even if very large, is finite, it can be argued that the possibility of a repetition of all events in a future time cannot be excluded.[51] To refute the theory, he made a shift from atoms to points in space, which allowed him, again, to introduce infinity as he required. He then argues that the probability of such an event taking place is 'computable en cero'.[52] This curious expression[53] is outside current Spanish-speaking scientific parlance, suggesting Borges imported it from a foreign text. A similar argument is used in several instances in 'Pierre Menard, autor del Quijote'[54] and in 'El inmortal'.[55]

Fix points, that is, points which return to themselves after a number of evolutions or transformations (which may be infinite in number), appear in a number of stories in different forms. One of these stories is that of a searcher who ends up discovering he was looking for himself.[56] An interesting variation is that of the killing of the Irish patriot Fergus Kilpatrick: the British police could not find the killer, perhaps because his killing was ordered by it. However, knowing an attempt on his life was being organised by a traitor, Kilpatrick ordered an investigation, which discovered that he was the traitor: his friends

---

[48]   J. L. Borges, *Historia de la eternidad*.

[49]   'los quebrados'.

[50]   In addition to Cantor's non-continuous one-to-one correspondence, Rey Pastor offered, in *Introducción a la Matemática Superior*, the example of Peano-Hilbert's continous, but not one-to-one, correspondence between a segment and a square

[51]   An original formulation of a similar argument was developed by Adolfo Bioy Casares in *La Invención de Morel*, 1940

[52]   J L Borges, *Historia de la eternidad*, p 80

[53]   The expression 'computable en cero' [computable at zero] is also used in 'La biblioteca de Babel', in J. L Borges, *Ficciones*

[54]   J. L. Borges, 'Pierre Menard, autor del Quijote', in *Ficciones* (Buenos Aires: Emecé, 1956).

[55]   J L. Borges, 'El inmortal', in *El Aleph* (Buenos Aires: Emecé, 1957), pp 20-22.

[56]   As, for example, in 'El acercamiento a Almotásim', in *Ficciones*

were forced to sentence him to death.[57]

The question of the direction of time is again discussed in the erudite essay *Historia de la eternidad*. Borges was certainly impressed by high-level structures capable of capturing infinite variety in a single element. Eternity becomes for him the time of all times as Aleph[58] was the point of all points. He also makes reference to the word or symbol that contains all languages:[59] the symbol of all symbols. Mirrors, dreams and chess games[60] are considered as a sort of general 'algebras' of abstract symbols: the potential containers of infinitely different possible libraries,[61] images or games.

Paradoxes on sets appear in other stories, such as 'Una rosa amarilla'.[62] In 'La lotería en Babilonia'[63] Borges makes an interesting twist: he introduces random decisions at each step of the process of the lottery, not just at the draw. It reads like a very realistic description of Argentine bureaucracy for anyone who may have had the privilege of experiencing it!

Crime fiction serves as an illustration of an abstract structure. It can be made concrete as a game, as a statement in algebra or as a proof of a theorem of geometry. In this sense a crime fiction work is a statement in a special form of language: it is an isolated universe with well defined rules. Once the basic elements are given, the causal chain leading to the solution of the mystery must be rigorously constructed, consistent with the rules of the game, well defined. If the plot is genuine, total, then the end of the chain, that is, the solution of the mystery, must be necessary. It must pass through all given facts and, if possible, lead to a unique solution of the mystery.

In 'La muerte y la brújula',[64] Borges carefully mounts such a structure, with death flowing through the vertex of a rhombus. If other Borges crime fiction stories can be described as algebraic this one is arithmetic: proportions, rather than empty containers of interchangeable objects, dominate. At the end of the story the detective Erik Lönnrot proposes to the serial murderer a linear labyrinth for his next crime. As he says, this is one in which many philosophers, and not only a mere detective, have been lost. He is right in saying so: the

---

[57]   J L Borges, 'Tema del traidor y del héroe'.

[58]   Aleph, the first letter of the Hebrew alphabet, is the symbol used by Cantor to designate any infinite set the elements of which can be put, one to one, into correspondence with the set of integer numbers.

[59]   In 'Parábola del Palacio', in J. L. Borges, *El hacedor* (Buenos Aires· Emecé, 1967), pp 59-60.

[60]   For example in 'El reloj de arena', in *El hacedor*, pp. 79 and 81 respectively.

[61]   On relations between sets and their elements, Borges says: 'Los individuos y las cosas existen en cuanto participan de la especie que los incluye, que es su realidad permanente' [Individuals and things exist in so far as they participate in the species that includes them, which is their permanent reality (*Historia de la eternidad*, p. 18.)]

[62]   J. L. Borges, *El hacedor*, p. 46 The question here is whether books are a mirror of the world (a set of all sets) or something added to it, that is, another element

[63]   J L Borges, *Ficciones*

[64]   J. L. Borges, 'La muerte y la brújula' [Death and the Compass], in *Ficciones*.

scheme of points he proposes is made of the first four points of Zeno's paradox of the arrow.

Conclusions

I have discussed briefly the state of ideas about space, time, matter and infinity in Argentina up to the early 1920s, that is, before the main pieces of Borges using these notions were written. I have also attempted to show that these ideas did not remain confined to the close circle of specialists. Through a unique alliance between science and literature forged in the Argentina of the 1870s, they penetrated the substantially much larger area of the educated, non-scientific, Buenos Aires of the time.

By the 1930s these ideas began to acquire, in some circles of Argentina, an autonomous identity which started to be transferred to literature. Borges's invasion of the innumerable, together with timely intensely personal biographical notes and digressions, gave his abstract fiction a unique sense of humanity and reality. Borges's appeal to these abstract structures seems to have been an instrument to express the infinite complexity of the world of reality and of the world of the spirit, the impossibility of total storage and the need for an intelligent element in it if its information is to become manageable. In some way, these ideas allowed Borges to express beautifully the difficulty of apprehending these worlds, their randomness and their volatile contingency.

Afterword
Borges and the Art of Allusion

Malcolm Bowie

The short stories of Borges are the work of a 'library cormorant', an erudite fantasist, a scholarly *bricoleur*, a cosmopolitan traveller whose magic carpet is woven from other people's words. In the postscript to 'El inmortal' [The Immortal], the narrator and Cartaphilus, the protagonist whom he quotes, reach a last moment of unanimity on this theme:

> A mi entender, la conclusión es inadmisible. *Cuando se acerca el fin,* escribió Cartaphilus, *ya no quedan imágenes del recuerdo; sólo quedan palabras.* Palabras, palabras desplazadas y mutiladas, palabras de otros, fue la pobre limosna que le dejaron las horas y los siglos (*El aleph*, p. 26).

> [In my opinion, such a conclusion is inadmissible. 'When the dawn draws near', wrote Cartaphilus, 'these no longer remain any remembered images; only words remain.' Words, displaced and mutilated words, words of others, were the poor pittance left him by the hours and the centuries] (*Labyrinths*, p. 149).[1]

The voices of these two fictional characters, poised in their shared final cadence, encapsulate an entire dimension of what might be termed 'the Borges voice'. He speaks quietly, but he speaks inside a whispering gallery. He takes pride in his rejection of rhetoric and fine writing, yet by way of his allusions and citations he inserts himself into an extended community of fellow writers and gives his own prose its constant air of plenitude. Language is all we have, Borges seems often to be saying, but it can scarcely be called a possession, for it is always on loan from other people, slips between our fingers as we put it to use, and insists on purveying other meanings than those we intend. The art of fiction, for Borges, is the art of negotiating between existing texts and of hybridising real texts and imaginary ones: it involves acknowledging that the human voice is composite, occasional, handed-down, haunted by the sound of past vocal inflections. The writer of fiction has the unenviable task of making something new from other people's litter.

Yet if we confine our attention solely to this aspect of Borges, and think of the reader's main pleasurable activity as that of burrowing down into the

---

[1] J L Borges, *Obras completas* (Buenos Aires: Emecé, 1970); *Labyrinths* (Harmondsworth: Penguin Books, 1970).

intertextual subsoil of his writings, we shall begin to lose contact with another distinctive dimension of his work, which is that of conspiracies, blood-feuds, military dishonour and violent death. From 'Hombre de la esquina rosada' ['Man from the Pink Corner'] (1933) to 'El encuentro' ['The Meeting'] (1969), his tales look out from the library into a neighbouring world of gauchos and outlaws, treachery and heroism, rifle-shots and slashing knives. 'I seem to be telling the same story over and over again', Borges wrote of 'El encuentro', and the underlying story-type which is repeatedly reincarnated is one in which an insistent interweaving of literary texts is suddenly arrested and transfixed by a reported mortal blow. 'El encuentro' itself brings together a number of allusions – to Lugones, to the Uruguayan ballads of Elías Regules, to Shakespeare's *Macbeth,* and to Borges's own hyper-allusive *El aleph* (1945) ['The Aleph']² – yet concerns itself, in its culminating moments, with daggers and torn flesh: knives have a life of their own, the narrator says, and the human beings who wield them are merely their temporary instruments. The literary text looks outwards from its own world of short-lived verbal effects, from that death of meaning without which, in literature, there is no life of meaning, towards that 'otra muerte' [other death] which no text can contain or tame. Literature looks to a world that is forever beyond its grasp and forever its undoing.

A tension of this kind sets Borges's brief fictions apart from that entire Western tradition of literary self-consciousness which found perhaps its last major representative and publicist in the person of Paul Valéry (1875-1945), and the comparison between the two writers is an instructive one. Borges now draws close to Valéry, and now takes his distance from him. In 'Pierre Menard, autor del Quijote' (1938),³ the narrator reports the discovery, among Menard's literary remains, of 'Una trasposición en alejandrinos del *Cimetière marin,* de Paul Valéry (*N R.F.,* enero de 1928)' ['A transposition into alexandrines of Paul Valery's *Le cimetière marin* (*N.R.F.,* January 1928)]. (*Labyrinths,* p. 64). This project is in its way almost as bold as Menard's main artistic endeavour, the recomposition – 'palabra por palabra y línea por línea' – of the *Quijote* itself. For Valéry had heroically resisted the temptations of the Alexandrine and, in writing his ambitious meditation on time, death, and intellectual responsibility, had returned to the antiquated decasyllabic line. This was the metre of the *Chanson de Roland* and it brought an after-echo of the French national epic, and a new air of heroism, into the very textures of Valéry's verse. Menard, by undoing Valéry's work and adding gratuitous syllables to his line, will have assimilated *Le Cimetière marin* to the lesser epic experiments of Lamartine, Vigny and Hugo.

The mischievous wit with which Borges here characterises the grandiose ambitions of Valéry and other European writers is to be seen again in his brief essay on 'Valéry as Symbol'. The distinguished man of letters to whom Borges pays tribute is altogether admirable in that he 'illustriously personifies the

---

²   *The Aleph and Other Stories, 1953-1969* (London. Picador, 1973).
³   *Ficciones.*

labyrinths of the mind' and 'magnifies the virtues of the mind', but at the same time he is limited by an odd disbelief in the power of fiction. *La Soirée chez M. Teste* would have given us, in its central character, 'one of the myths of our time' if only Valéry had not made him into a mouthpiece for his own views and his own flattering self-images. The contrast between Borges and Valéry is striking, for all the allusiveness and literary self-consciousness they seem at first to have in common. Where Valéry recoils in fastidious distaste from the art of the mere story-teller, Borges revels in it, embedding stories within other stories and finding incitements to further fiction-making at every turn. Where Valéry seeks after a new capacious selfhood in which thought can unfold beauteously, self-delightingly and at leisure, Borges disperses selfhood across a cast of characters and gives impediments to thinking a role in each of his tiny dramas. Where Valéry's labyrinths are internal to 'une pensée qui se pense' [a thought which thinks itself], those of Borges hover undecidably between the inner and outer worlds, and between the possibility and the impossibility of thought. Valéry is enchanted by the myth of Narcissus; Borges is not. Valéry could (and did) write: 'Mon imagination ne se meut jamais sur le plan humain moyen commun, c'est-à-dire, en se plaçant *in medios homines* dans l'univers des échanges ...' [My imagination never moves about on the average and ordinary human plane, that is to say, posing itself in *in medios homines* in the world of exchange]; Borges could not have written anything of the kind.

It is not my intention to disparage Valéry, but simply to point out how very different the two writers are and to draw attention to the compactedness and power of implication that each of the great Borges stories possesses. Each of these stories is built upon a conceit, but the author himself could not be less conceited. He offers his reader infinite learning worn infinitely lightly. Borges inhabits literature as one might inhabit a great city – surprised by its curiosities, pausing at its crossroads, crossing and recrossing its thoroughfares endlessly, switching from its surface to its underground routes, and never wanting it to be a single portentous thing. His stories often present themselves as the after-shocks triggered by earlier upheavals of the literary imagination or as the fore-shocks of a *livre à venir*.

Borges makes a story by itemising Pierre Menard's unpublished *œuvre*, by reviewing an imaginary novel, *El acercamiento a Almotásim* [The Approach to Al-Mu'tasim], from an imaginary Bombay barrister, or by placing himself under the joint influence of Chesterton and Leibniz, in 'Tema del traidor y del héroe' [Theme of the Traitor and the Hero], in order to sketch a possible plot for a possible future work. 'El Aleph' is cast as a mocking tribute to a bad poet, the memory of whose pretentious and banal works is, for the narrator, also a memory of Shakespeare, Hobbes, Dante, Homer, Hesiod, Goldoni and countless other writers of long-standing celebrity. But at the visionary climax of the work, induced in the narrator by the good offices of the bad poet, literature is exquisitely reminded of its limitations. The Aleph is the point in space and time where all objects, events and epochs co-exist while retaining their singularity; it is the All contracted into a single, many-mansioned sign:

vi en un traspatio de la calle Soler las mismas baldosas que hace treinta
años vi en el zaguán de una casa en Fray Bentos, vi racimos, nieve,
tabaco, vetas de metal, vapor de agua, vi convexos desiertos
ecuatoriales y cada uno de sus granos de arena, vi en Inverness a una
mujer que no olvidaré, vi la violenta cabellera, el altivo cuerpo, vi un
cáncer en el pecho, vi un círculo de tierra seca en una vereda, donde
antes hubo un árbol, vi una quinta de Adrogué, un ejemplar de la
primera versión inglesa de Plinio, la de Philemon Holland, vi a un
tiempo cada letra de cada página... (*El aleph*, p. 165).

[in an inner patio in the Calle Soler I saw the same paving tile I had
seen thirty years before in the entranceway to a house in the town of
Fray Bentos; I saw clusters of grapes, snow, tobacco, veins of metal,
steam; I saw convex equatorial deserts and every grain of sand in them;
I saw a woman at Inverness whom I shall not forget; I saw her violent
switch of hair, her proud body, I saw a cancer in her breast; I saw a
circle of dry land in a sidewalk where formerly there had been a tree; I
saw a villa in Adrogué; I saw a copy of the first English version of
Pliny, by Philemon Holland, and saw simultaneously every letter on
every page... (*A Personal Anthology*, p. 149)].[4]

The city of literature is here, down to the last letter of Holland's Pliny, but
then so are cities proper – Buenos Aires, Fray Bentos, Adrogué and Inverness;
literary labour is here, but then so are leisure, ease and rapture. Having been
deprived of its privileged status and diplomatic immunity by the egalitarian
inclusiveness of the Aleph, literature is partially restored to its former dignity in
the postscript to the tale: 'Por increíble que parezca, yo creo que hay (o que
hubo) otro Aleph, yo creo que el Aleph de la calle Garay era un falso Aleph'
[Incredible as it may seem, I believe there is (or was) another Aleph, I believe
that the Aleph in the Calle Garay was a false Aleph] If the Aleph is indeed a
fake, and if the ecstatic sense of ubiquity that is produces in the beholder is the
by-product of delusion and wish-fulfilment, then it takes its place – precariously,
for a doubt remains – in the archive of fakes, the sublime cabinet of delusions,
that is called art. Borges's story hesitates on the threshold between art and that
which exceeds and overrides it. A tragic sense of art's final impotence is woven
into this portrait of its magical powers in action.

No more moving account of the writer as threshold-dweller is to be found in
Borges's works than 'El milagro secreto' ['The Secret Miracle'] (1943). A
Jewish writer, Jaromir Hladík, is allowed a miraculous suspension of time, in
which to complete his last work, before a firing-squad murders him. Borges
synchronises the tale of Hladík's last-minute artistic triumph with one of his own
finest effects of art:

Dio término a su drama: no le faltaba ya resolver sino un solo epíteto.

---

[4]   *A Personal Anthology by Jorge Luis Borges* (London. Picador, 1973)

Lo encontró; la gota de agua resbaló en su mejilla. Inició un grito enloquecido, movió la cara, la cuádruple descarga lo derribó (*Ficciones*, p. 167).

[He concluded his drama. He had only the problem of a single phrase. He found it. The drop of water slid down his cheek. He opened his mouth in a maddened cry, moved his face, dropped under the quadruple blast (*Labyrinths*, p. 124)].

As Hladík's missing epithet falls into place, a raindrop that had fallen on his face, immediately before his divinely ordained reprieve, turns into a tear. An unutterable sorrow has found literary expression. But these are not the last words of the story. The story ends upon a documentary note, a *fait divers*:

Jaromir Hladík murió el veintinueve de marzo, a las nueve y dos minutos de la mañana (*Ficciones*, p. 167).

[Jaromir Hladík died on 29 March at 9.02 a.m. (*Labyrinths*, p. 124)].

The final effect of art involves the removal of art from the scene. The unutterable horror of the Nazi genocide has the last word; and the allusive fabric of the literary text is turned again towards that which is forever extrinsic to it.

In the last sentence of his tribute to Valéry, Borges spoke of those 'chaotic idols of blood, earth and passion' to which Valéry always preferred 'the lucid pleasures of thought'. What is so remarkable about the art of allusion as practised by Borges is that the pleasures of thought, and erudition, and literary *bricolage* should be pursued in full knowledge of the bloody, earthy and impassioned affairs of men. Borges writes *in medios homines*, in a world where knives slash, guns fire and men bleed. The wit, the allusiveness, the literary self-absorption of his texts are shot through with a remorseless awareness of cruelty and death. Death, in particular, in its action-at-a-distance upon the literary text, confers tragic grandeur upon these economical, understated and plainly written fictions. They are intricately self-referring verbal constructions which yet have the power to refer their readers outwards to a world in which they no longer read but merely live and die.

Printed in the USA
CPSIA information can be obtained
at www.ICGtesting.com
JSHW060339070224
56800JS00005B/33

9 781900 039215